11 21

Woods-Working Women

Woods-Working

Elaine Pitt Enarson

Women

Sexual
Integration
in the
U.S. Forest Service

The University of Alabama Press

Title page photograph by Lawrence M. Shaffield

Library of Congress Cataloging in Publication Data

Enarson, Elaine Pitt, 1949–
    Woods-working women.

    Bibliography: p.
    Includes index.
    1. United States. Forest Service—Officials and
employees. 2. Women—Employment—United States.
3. Affirmative action programs—United States. 4. Forest
reserves—Oregon. I. Title.
SD565.E5 1984   331.4'133   83-6725
ISBN 0-8173-0188-7

For Evan

Contents

Preface

This book is intended as a portrait of women and men working together in the nation's forests, where women are slowly integrating work crews and workplaces once exclusively male. I have approached issues in occupational structure and social change in a personal way, locating the substance and significance of social structure in the details of everyday life. My focus is on interaction and emotion at work and on the ambiguities of the firsthand, first-person story. Women are learning to work in new ways and places, so the story is largely theirs to tell, though coworkers and bosses, lovers, and husbands all add their point of view.

Understanding the spirit of this process of integration meant talking with those most directly touched, and this work exploits the methodology of the focused interview.[1] Most interviews were conducted after work, in private homes. Often we sat around woodstoves or fireplaces, in cabins and trailers facing rivers or mountain clearings in the Oregon woods. The interviews stretched from late fall 1978 through the winter and spring of 1979 and into the beginning of the summer season. These were people most hospitable and gracious, usually eager to talk, always generous with time and coffee, and by and large not easily intimidated by tape-recording. They gave careful consideration to topics not always pleasant or familiar, turned out animals and turned off chiming clocks, and sometimes even packed off the family for the evening. Protecting their confidence is a major consideration in the preparation of this report.[2]

Interviewing is no more free from intellectual and personal bias than other aspects of research. Intellectual bias can be identified and acknowledged; with respect to personal bias the researcher can only hope to guard against blinders, prejudice, and self-delusion. This book is the result of my collaboration with those who watch the sun rise in the forest each workday morning, but I was a professional outsider, and my perspective prevails. The discussion, interpretation, and analysis proceed generally in my terms.

Transcribing tapes months later, I heard again the interruptions of the curious husband, suddenly thirsty and passing through, the crackling fire, and the whizzing log trucks, and it would all come back. I recalled the faces and laughs and puzzlement, diffidence turning to assertion, distance becoming warmth, the mood of the night, and the farewell. In the homes of the men as much as the women, my reception was always warm. While my voice dominates analytically here, in my memory it is their faces, their words, and their feelings which linger.

It is impossible to convey the richness and complexity of each of the lives glimpsed in action here, to show the humor and patience, bitterness, ambivalence, and faith which in turn color women's lives working with men in the woods. To make sense of small private events in the political and historical context lending them significance demands some degree of objectification. The task is to convey and yet move beyond the gripping immediacy of the shouting match and tears, the laughter and the embraces in the woods. History and biography are constituted in the first instance by such small scenarios, and analysis of the social world begins here, preserving always the human experience of history and social structure—the private troubles of contemporary social issues, as C. Wright Mills put it. This is the cornerstone of the sociological imagination, and it guides this study of occupational change.

The research upon which this work builds was partially supported by a Woodrow Wilson Doctoral Dissertation Grant in Women's Studies and an American Association of University Women Fellowship. The Department of Sociology at the University of Oregon and members of my family provided additional financial support. I gratefully acknowledge this assistance, without which the project could never have been completed.

The U.S. Forest Service helped in many ways to see the research through to completion, and I am grateful for its interest and assistance. My greatest debt, of course, is to the women and men who shared their time and thoughts with me and made possible a few answers to some big questions. I hope I have done them justice.

I am immeasurably indebted in altogether different ways to others: to my parents, Harold and Audrey Enarson, who taught me to care; to Joan Acker, Don Van Houten, and David Wellman for helping me recognize the important questions, to the staff and students of the Department of Sociology who always believed this book possible; and especially to Carl Hering and to Kate Barry, who shared it all.

Woods-Working Women

1

Introduction

This book takes a firsthand look into the problems and prospects of women woods workers in the Forest Service in two Oregon national forests. While increasingly women join men in their work, we know little of how sexual integration shapes the daily working lives of those on the forefront of social change.[1] Analyzing the process of change clarifies the forces both maintaining and undermining occupational sex segregation and traditional relations between the sexes.

We will look in detail at the human story of one of the many affirmative action plans in practice today, from the point of view of those most personally engaged in it. The book explores concrete daily interaction in a context of change and contradiction, as "wrong" workers join traditionally correct ones. Women in the woods, like women preachers and pilots, have much to teach us. Through their stories we may grasp how sex segregation at work is made real, interpreted and contradicted, challenged and affirmed.

Women doing "men's work" are still very rare, of course, but when pioneers do move into traditionally male jobs they challenge important barriers. These first steps are important not because they open new horizons for a privileged few—and they do—but because they are part of a larger, more complex process of change. We live in a world rigidly stratified by gender, so strikingly evident in the labor force, where four of every five women work in the white and pink-collar ghettos of the female work world. Indeed, the trend is toward increasing sex segregation at work.[2]

In addition, the internal labor market profoundly structures women's participation within each occupational category or organization, shaping internal patterns of segregation, including modes of organizational au-

1

thority, sexual composition of work groups, professional specialties, segregation by firm within single industries, even physical boundaries of
location within work settings.[3] Challenging these patterns concretely
broadens some women's choices, clarifies the inner dynamics of segregation, and ultimately helps us see the importance of the sharing between
women and men of all kinds of work. The sexual division of labor must be
understood to be effectively challenged. Only when no corner of human
activity, no expression of human possibility, is limited to half the world
can we begin to build a future challenging and satisfying for us all.[4]

Two major themes dominate this analysis of affirmative action in
forestry. One focus is on the sexual relations of production, specifically
the sexualizing of work relations with women in integrated workplaces,
and women's response in turn. Historically, this theme shapes women's
daily working lives, and the perception of women in predominantly
sexual terms continues to influence female employment patterns.[5] Opposition to work placing women and men in close proximity has a long
history.[6] Complaints and worries about on-the-job romance are a staple
item in the advice columns, from women and men alike. Contemporary
accounts of women in nontraditional occupations invariably raise the
specter of sexual or romantic entanglement.[7] One airline pilot, for instance, makes the charming argument that cockpit intimacy might lead
to affairs between male and female pilots, thus endangering public
safety. He urges that only unattractive women be hired as commercial
pilots.[8] On the other hand, an administrator at the National Aeronautics
and Space Administration, commenting on women's role in space, notes
that male astronauts are like "other normal human beings, they'd want
sexual diversion" during long stays in space.[9] The sexualizing of the
integrated workplace demands examination if we are to move beyond
this level of analysis of the sexual relations of production.

A second major focus is how women newcomers affect the job itself. A
major theme in the history of resistance to women in male-dominated
jobs is the protection of intrinsic working conditions; the job skills, degree
of control possible over the work process, kinds of social relations possible, and cultural definitions of work and workers are all important to
work satisfaction and job prestige.[10] The prevailing identity of work and
workers as especially "masculine" goes a long way in determining relative
status, and there is every reason to believe that workers will protect
whatever bits and pieces of self-respect and autonomy their work affords
them.[11] If integration appears to threaten valued aspects of the job, male
workers will resist women co-workers with every resource at their command.[12] This study examines such sources of resistance in some detail.

Change in the organization of work and in the sexual relations of production is most apparent when women begin to join in especially valued male work, as here resistance is likely to be strong. Thus, while women in a nontraditional field like forestry are very much a minority of all employed women, their experiences teach us a great deal about the general process of organizational change and sexual integration. Particularly masculine occupations highlight these themes, many of which color the experiences of other pioneers in the coal mines, construction fields, fire stations, and army barracks around the nation.

The Forest Service encompasses a variety of typically masculine and male-dominated jobs, from tree planting to fire fighting. While most wilderness trail guards in the Forest Service would yield to a choker setter on a logging crew, Forest Service workers at all levels do consider themselves woodsmen, ranking high on the symbolic scale of manliness. In the Northwest particularly, the Paul Bunyan ethos colors the lives of all those working in the woods, not just the legendary flannel-shirted lumberjacks. The organization also affords access to a growing pool of women working alongside men in the woods, clearing trails, lighting slash fires, planning roads, and marking timber cuts. Indeed, the two national forests employing those who speak out in this book share a reputation for leadership in minority hiring and devote considerable organizational resources to encouraging nontraditional workers.[13]

Examination of sexual integration in forestry, then, brings into sharp focus the dynamics of the status quo and the mechanisms of its defense and challenge. Ultimately this case study of woods-working women suggests that male co-workers do attempt control over female integration through a variety of mechanisms, including dominance in tasks most dangerous and physically demanding and defense of a gratifying masculine work culture. The female challenge to male and masculine work is also managed through the sexualizing of women co-workers and relations at work, and the negotiation of models of relationship acceptable to men. Male control is far from monolithic, however, facing challenge from female newcomers through both organizational and personal strategies, including ridicule and alliance, formal grievance, and informal feminist organizing. Prospects for meaningful and lasting sexual integration of outdoor jobs in the Forest Service are rooted in larger organizational trends and in the gradual undermining of the visibility and vulnerability of the token woman. These and other lessons from the front lines enhance our understanding of the challenge ahead.

2

The Context of Change

The 1970s brought small changes in the sex structure of the labor force and great public debate over the pace and propriety of what seemed always to be much larger changes. Feminist theory combined with the daily experiences of masses of employed women to focus attention on the situation of the new working woman. Typically, this focus meant agitation to expand job opportunities, principally in the white-collar world of business and the professions, but also integration of apprenticeships and union shops of the skilled crafts and trades. The emphasis on women in men's jobs has always been disproportionate, however. The media love the chic business woman and the glowing telephone linewoman, but have tended to overlook—until the recent discovery of the male secretary— the more common pattern of men entering such traditional female occupations as elementary school teaching or social work.[1] "Affirmative action" became a code phrase describing the intrusion of women into male lines of work, freely associated with the "lowering of standards" and "reverse discrimination," and was challenged in the courts and in casual conversation alike. Yet government agencies like the U.S. Forest Service began to feel the impact of women's new ambitions.

Like other organizations, the Forest Service has always hired women. Matching the "right person to the right job" fairly demands women workers in certain positions around the office. Indeed, many men in the Forest Service can recall the time when women were only clerical workers (and clerical workers were only women) and can relate the details of the arrival of the first insurgents—women with hard hats and a yen for the woods. Inasmuch as one-third of all wage-earning women perform clerical work, and the government is the largest single employer of women, it is not surprising to find women dominating the clerical series in the

4

Forest Service. They meet the public, handle the voluminous paperwork, and smooth over tensions with a smile—and sometimes still with a cup of coffee. Extremely limited mobility and low wages are their reward for loyalty, competence, and the stress of full-time clerical work. They begin now to regard field work differently, and a few make the transition from office to field work through job training programs. But most woods-working women are new to the Forest Service.

What kind of an outfit do they join, when women "come on board" with the Forest Service? The agency can be described as a conservative, hierarchical, and bureaucratic organization, richly colored by a military ethos and imbued with a certain masculine culture.[2] One of the oldest federal agencies, chartered under President Roosevelt in 1905, its burgeoning scale and scope during the century were characteristic of the time. It expanded rapidly to tasks far beyond the original mandate of fire control and conservation, now employing soil scientists, wildlife biologists, geologists, sociologists, and all manner of timber and fire specialists. In an era of restricted federal employment and tight budgets, the tide of specialization may be turning, as highly specialized workers are expensive. Still, with a permanent labor force of more than 37,000 nationally, the Forest Service remains a major employer both of professionals in forestry and related fields and of semiskilled manual woods workers. In addition, it supports a broad labor force through contract work ranging from environmental impact study to tree planting. The national trend toward managing jobs now contracted out to the private sector complements the trends toward specialization and professionalization.

Entrenched in the powerful Department of Agriculture, the Forest Service plays a role in forest management and timber production that gives it great clout nationally. Furthermore it is often also the major employer in remote areas. Its role in timber management, especially in the Northwest, makes the woods products industry a close partner, creating an intimacy which is sometimes controversial. Increasingly, the Forest Service finds itself drawn into battle over issues that suddenly inspire public debate—herbicide use, the designation of wilderness areas, mining rights, even the traditional commitment to preventing wildfires. The two national forests considered here are particularly powerful because they are major producers within the heavily timbered region. Foresters throughout the nation compete for professional jobs here, where there is opportunity for recognition and promotion. Also available are the money and security to indulge in experimental programs, including affirmative action, and the forests enjoy a reputation for tolerance and innovation in employment.

Administratively, the Forest Service is complex. It manages a variety of rich public resources, from water and range to historic sites, coordinates the use of state and private lands, and maintains semiautonomous research laboratories. The basic administrative unit is the national forest, divided geographically and administratively into a number of districts or engineering zones. Some national forests encompass national recreation areas, supervise Job Corps centers, oversee youth work projects (e.g., Young Adult Conservation Corps), and occasionally manage a seed and tree nursery as well. The many and varied activities are coordinated by a forest supervisor. The national forests form part of any one of nine national regions (the Northwest Region, for example, includes nineteen national forests in two states), supervised by a regional forester, and ultimately the nerve center in Washington, D.C. Career foresters eventually fill specialized staff and administrative positions of increasing distance from the daily work of the field crews, moving from the national forest district level to the more remote supervisor's and regional offices. This study focuses on those at the lowest rungs of the organizational ladder—the women and men (including their supervisors and the district ranger) who earn their living performing the routine manual, outdoor work of resource management.

Though many workers never leave their hometowns, entering the Forest Service means joining an organization with a strong national as well as local profile. Each administrative unit—from the regional offices to the most isolated range and experiment stations—develops an independence of spirit and character, as do the national forests. Like families within a neighborhood, these units quarrel, gossip, and struggle for power and attention. At the national forest level, jurisdictional boundaries between districts are often very strictly drawn, and forest and regional boundaries are sometimes never crossed. The authority and prestige of the agency are fiercely defended against such poor cousins as the state departments of forestry or other federal agencies.

Most ambitious workers will change jobs, for transfer within and between national forests is encouraged and is required for mid-level promotion. In this way it is hoped that loyalty attaches to the organization rather than to the local community. The lure of local influence is minimized by this calculated rootlessness. Still, local traditions and identity are deep-rooted, and the influence of the unit managers in local communities is considerable. Rangers facetiously comment that their professional organization, the Society of American Foresters, might equally well be called "A Loose Association of Absolute Monarchs." The requirement of mobility has recently been extended to unit managers. Five of seven rangers in one national forest changed jobs in one recent three-year period; in the past their tenure at one post might have stretched through decades.

In the Northwest, the tasks associated with timber production and fire control—from collecting seed cones to "mopping up" controlled burns— dominate the agenda and thus the workdays of most workers, "timber beasts" and environmentalists alike. Workers are needed in timber management to assess the quality and quantity of timber stands, to monitor the need for thinning or planting, to estimate board feet of marketable timber, and to maintain water and soil quality. When timber sales are held, sale boundaries must be marked, access roads must be sited and cost estimated, and staff reports on environmental impacts must be prepared. Generally, professional engineers supervise construction projects, and professional foresters manage timber sales; recreation management also employs a number of technicians and professionals. The field crews include hands-on technical workers (engineering and forest technicians) and their working supervisors, backed by professionals who manage the growing administrative burden and provide specialized expertise—the timber sale officer, the fire safety officer, and the soil scientist, for example.

In addition, all workers are trained routinely in fire safety and fire fighting, though most will never fight a wildfire. Any Forest Service worker may be called upon when necessary. Some fire control workers will join regional teams of highly trained and mobile crews on call for work around the region and country. Others include the famous "smokejumpers" and helicopter rappellers, who are flown into remote fires in inaccessible terrain. But the major task is to prepare and conduct controlled fires that rid the woods of hazardous logging slash. Some workers engage in public education or drive the water pumper trucks needed to "plumb" the unit to be burned, but most low-level technicians, male or female, spend the season piling slash and burning it. In the Northwest, fire control is the major seasonal employer, swelling the ranks of the temporaries each summer with two and three times the usual work force.

Most of the people who speak out in this book are employed as survey or forest technicians, assigned to various departments at the discretion of the unit manager. In 1981 in Region VI, women were 13 percent of all forest and all engineering technicians. Women today join men in the routine work of piling slash, marking timber, or walking survey lines. Like most male Forest Service workers, few are professionals (only 3 percent nationwide in 1977); all of the professionals in this sample who oversee timber sales or manage forest fires are men. While women account for 17 percent of all technicians nationwide, they are just 8 percent of the professional workers in the Forest Service. Of every five

new workers in entry-level technician slots nationwide in 1980, two were
women; and of all those working in the lowest ranks (GS 1–5), 60 percent
were female.[3]

The women woods workers represented here are predominantly
"ground stompers" trying to be "just one of the guys" on a crew of five to
ten and are typically one of only two women on the crew. An occasional
crew is evenly divided by sex, and some districts occasionally pair off one
woman and one man in working partnerships. Newcomers to a job, male
or female, need training initially, and because there are fewer experienced women, most will work most directly with men. Occasionally, a
district creates an all-female crew, but they are increasingly rare. Rather,
women tend to be distributed throughout the crews and departments. As
we shall see, this constant minority status has many ramifications. One
consequence is that women already isolated by their small numbers feel
doubly removed from one another and cannot easily provide the support
that many want and need.[4] This book focuses on female-male interaction
predominantly, just as it is female-male relations that color women woods
workers' daily work lives.

We shall see that departments and districts vary in attitude toward
women in nontraditional work. Women field workers can now be found
in virtually every department. When weather forces them to retreat
indoors, they may also be asked to perform administrative, maintenance, or housekeeping chores. Moving between and within districts
and national forests exposes workers to different supervisors and departments, to varied work conditions and terrain, and thus to new kinds
of skills and job opportunities. Committed workers eventually specialize
somewhat and pursue careers in one or another aspect of the agency's
work.

Most of the work of the Forest Service has traditionally been performed by men and carries all of them—professional and technician
alike—outside periodically on days rainy and fine. They climb hillsides,
slosh through creeks, struggle with chain saws, and generally tend the
public's land. Such work is now largely done by temporaries. While
"Smokey" has traditionally been a favorite with the public, the organization has not been immune to the impact of the shrinking public dollar
and growing hostility to government bureaucracy.

A number of consequences follow. As in many other government
agencies, employment levels in the Forest Service are maintained
through routine evasion of federally imposed job ceilings. According to a
kind of personnel shell game, a growing group of essentially full-time
workers do not appear on the rolls on the day when federally employed
heads are counted. These workers have irregular appointments, guaran-

teed only a set number of pay periods unless called back to work, as many are with regularity. Their jobs vary in stability, and many guarantee work and income comparable to those of full-time regular positions. Workers with longer tenure and regular permanent positions are now a relatively privileged group, inclined to hedge their bets and protect their jobs.

The dramatic growth in "temporary" seasonal workers, however, is perhaps the most important consequence of the limited number of federal jobs. This new class of workers is now fully entrenched, although there was always in the past a more limited need for temporary labor. Many temporaries work a six-month season or longer, sharing in some of the benefits of the regular workers. Their status as transients is fixed; although they may return year after year, perhaps to the same job, department, and district, many feel they remain "just a temporary, just a body."

The growing reliance on temporaries, including professional part-timers, is controversial. They come cheaper, but their attitudes and commitment often reflect what they see as cavalier treatment by the government. They resent working hard for less pay, less security, and less respect. Disgruntled supervisors note the hidden costs of saving wages by hiring temporaries, including high turnover rates, the constant need for time-consuming and costly training, and the gradual erosion of the traditional reservoir of skilled, experienced, and committed workers.

While in the past, technicians were most often hired on as permanent workers, today they more commonly work several seasons before winning a permanent appointment. The agency employs a work force of more than 14,000 seasonal workers nationwide. In the current climate of re-trenchment, the enforced apprenticeship is longer, and competition for permanent jobs has grown especially steep. Women just entering forestry feel the full brunt of these obstacles. Yet their numbers have increased: in 1978, in Region VI, women accounted for 14.7 percent of all permanent technical and administrative workers, up from 7.4 percent six years earlier.[5] Nationwide, women's representation in these ranks increased from 12 percent to 22 percent between 1977 and 1981.[6] As more women "join up" each summer as temporary technicians—clearing trails and cleaning campgrounds, "stacking sticks" for slash burning, brushing survey lines for new roads, and walking wilderness trails—the pool of competitors for scarce permanent field jobs slowly broadens to include more women.

With the shift to contract work and thus to contract crew management, career progress increasingly reflects management skills rather than the technical expertise and field experience integral to traditional field work. Increased public demands for accountability and planning add to the agency's new sensitivity to the art of public relations. Even as its popularity on campus grows, forestry work is increasingly bureaucratic and professional; workers' hopes for time in the woods are increasingly frustrated by committees and reports. The familiar process of inflation in necessary educational credentials follows naturally.

The Forest Service is still dominated by "lifers" of an earlier generation who hold different skills and priorities, but the career field worker entering the ranks today will need professional training to progress. The nondegreed technician can hope to advance only into the ranks of the crew bosses. Only in fire control can workers still advance into high-level management jobs and this is increasingly difficult without professional credentials. Distinctions between permanent and temporary worker, and between management and field worker, undercut the unanimity of crew and district. Even more decisive is the distance between professional and technical workers. The internal labor market is sharply divided, with different educational credentials, routes of entry, career patterns, and eventual prospects for technicians and professionals. The key distinction is educational: all professionals are college educated, but until recently, most technicians were not. However, the two-year associate degree in forestry available at many community colleges is becoming essential, though not yet formally required, and many younger technicians have at least these two years of college.

There are parallel differences in personal style, demeanor, and all the subtleties of what is essentially a class distance. These are boundaries of organizational caste which the Civil Service conversion roster, intended to facilitate movement from technical to professional series, cannot begin to eliminate. The differences between the Eagle Scouts and the local boys, the temporaries and the "lifers," are as marked as the traditional gap between the "peons" and the "muckety mucks."

The Forest Service is also a self-consciously masculine organization.[7] Hardly the paragon of the wilderness man, nor perhaps even of the red-blooded logger, the male Forest Service worker remains distinct. His work makes him feel and seem more stereotypically masculine than, for example, his counterparts among bill collectors or the members of the American Sociological Association. This self-image is an element of organization life and daily interaction too rarely explored, though very relevant as women begin to share the workplace.

The dominant woods-working culture of the Northwest also colors organizational life. The tradition of forestry work shapes cultural life as much as it does the local economy and regional mortality statistics. The prevailing culture embodies many of the traditions of an enduring rural, working-class, woods-working life dominated by logging and mill work;

and it is country, straight or hip. It is to loggers that Forest Service men contrast themselves and are compared by others, often unfavorably. Managers compare their forest management practices with those of private timber companies. And the women of this study confront the dress, language, demeanor, and politics of woods-working men. Regardless of its personal resonance for individual workers, this cultural backdrop is important and is reflected in the politics, jokes, and arguments at work as much as in the music on the truck radio.

In many cases this is the natural culture of the women themselves, who are often the wives and daughters and granddaughters of Northwest woods-working families. They have shared in the pleasures and skills of the outdoor life of work and leisure and have brothers and sons much like their co-workers. To those who knew the corn fields of Iowa but never before saw an evergreen, or who easily negotiate downtown Chicago but not a standard transmission, this culture is a real challenge. For some it mediates a larger class difference, while for others it sums up the real meaning of "macho."

Male workers have often been in the woods in many different capacities, both hunting and logging, and may later take jobs with private timber companies or contractors. Though it is ruefully rejected by most as fantasy, irrelevant, and probably dysfunctional, the myth of the hypermasculine fire fighter lives on—"Superman-Macho flying through the air with the greatest of speed to put out the Great Forest Fire," as one ranger put it. Particularly "macho" sensibilities are selectively attributed—tobacco chewing and routine obscenity to men in some departments, "professional" demeanor elsewhere—in what amounts to an implicit class analysis. To some women the result is an essentially homosocial world in which men seek and value the company of men and women seem irrelevant much of the time.[8] One woman remarks of the men at work: "They're *into* men. You know, it's a macho—they're engineers, you know, very male-dominated. . . . They're willing to relate to women, but . . . they like to spend their time relating to men. It's like, maybe, one of the reasons they got into that job in the first place, you know, that they like working with men who are men."

For all the qualifications (and there are many), the women interviewed feel a decidedly militarist and masculine tone to field work and field workers. Without exactly being "strangers in a strange land," they do come abruptly face to face with this work culture when they join the Forest Service.

Traditionally, workers have been able to take pride in being government foresters, despite low wage levels and bureaucratic frustrations. For some—a shrinking number—there is reward enough in working for

Smokey, for an outfit they feel cares about its mission of protecting natural resources and looks out for the owl as well as for the timber. For some self-described "workers of conscience," wages are not as important. Though the environmental record may not be perfect, the Forest Service still represents "the good guys in the *dirty* white hats."

Some workers have had jobs with bigger paychecks in private industry that did not satisfy them. One burly young man is almost embarrassed to explain why he no longer works winters for the local timber company. He sees his job as a rare opportunity for "humankind to harvest and put back," in contrast to the lucrative but purposeless logging business of "raping the land." For him, there was no comparison between saying "Hey, I'm a logger," and "Hey, I'm happy." But this level of commitment is by no means universal, nor will it necessarily survive the new chilling public opinion of government work and workers or the attack on the conditions of federal employment.

The far-flung structure, relentless mobility, and strong local identities demand a unifying glue of some kind, and many things contribute to it. Organizational commitment and loyalty are encouraged by a shared creed (principally the prevention of fire), uniform, argot, and—not least—the symbolic Smokey-the-Bear imagery. Perhaps to facilitate the essential interchangeability of personnel, or perhaps because "like hires like," the careers of certain typical kinds of workers blossom. There develops a recognizable, stereotypical "Forest Service guy" appropriate to the various status levels.[9]

One aspect of this identity is militarism. The stereotypic "double-dipping" military retiree is not uncommon, and his presence reinforces the already pronounced military ethos of the Forest Service. This effect is evident especially in the fire organization, where many Vietnam veterans are found. It tends to be a hierarchical, authoritarian outfit characterized by a self-consciously militarist discipline and "esprit de corps." This coloration is extensive in the language and ways of all departments: people "join the Service," are mobilized and demobilized during fires, become "Forest Service wives," and so forth. Some departments and districts are known to be especially militarist. While the symbolism of long hair on men has largely eroded, it once kept some men out of jobs; today, opposition to women in nontraditional jobs is often attributed to this atmosphere.

In addition to these and other characteristic sentiments, a carefully constructed ideology of the organizational "family" prevails. Though some reject it, this mystical sense of shared purpose, interdependence, and commitment is widespread at the district level and is often deeply felt. The family, of course, is patriarchal, and the ranger's character and authority dominate. He and others may be serviced by a "Big Momma" (perhaps a long-time secretary or business management assistant) who organizes the swirl of social activities, carefully guards her turf, and manages the affective climate through "emotion work." (In one instance, she had all other women doing hand work for an expected baby of a Forest Service worker during lunch breaks.) And as in a family, a world of difference exists between the position and prospects of the various members; the district ranger, receptionist, professional forester, and seasonal technician all face profoundly different futures.

Notwithstanding the mothering and fathering, the countless potlucks and "keggers," and the shared affinity with Smokey and all he symbolizes, Forest Service workers in fact work in a hierarchical, rigidly stratified, conservative organization, and by and large they know it. The oldtimer puts it mildly when he stresses that "we're not a homogeneous group," for the organization is riddled with the tensions, jealousies, and conflicts of all those with different privileges and prospects.

The divisions run deep and are made painfully real in little ways every day. They are widely recognized—sometimes lamented, but generally expected and accepted. In contrast, the sexual barrier has been until recently nearly invisible, though it manifestly cuts as deeply and decisively as these other dimensions of privilege and prestige.

The Politics of Affirmative Action

When the battle was joined in the late 1960s, the Forest Service was a rigidly stratified organization with sexual boundaries of interaction, activity, and prospects as self-evident and accepted as the walls separating the work areas of the sexes. These boundaries are still evident, but they are no longer uncomplicated or unquestioned; in some ways, in fact, they are under siege. It is this sentiment which is important and not a bodycount index of change.

No longer the shock troops, women field workers today are a second generation of pioneers. They are both exceptional and routine. If the sight of braids under a hard hat no longer stops traffic (as it did once, for "in 1975, I mean, you were a *freak*"), in some quarters it is still remarkable. While rarely lumped together on all-women crews or confronted with men unfamiliar with women in the woods, these members of the Forest Service still work in extremely lopsided groups and face the problems of the solo woman and the female first. Paradoxically, there is some feeling that women are no longer a significant "minority," although they continue to be highly visible, clustered in marginal positions with uncertain futures, and subject to scrutiny and commentary around the districts and region. There is a sense of immense progress in the face of little substantive change which cannot easily be refuted by facts and figures: three women on a crew of twenty seem like "plenty" to those who look back rather than forward.

Professional women, too, can count on isolation. Women foresters (and biologists, engineers, or silviculturists) are still very rare and are often known to each other by name or reputation throughout the two forests and the region. Once employed, they enjoy a more privileged position than their female co-workers and subordinates. They are popular with unit managers as affirmative action "quotas." There is a certain competition for professional women in this climate, though the manager quoted below overstates the case: "Just get a degree in forestry and step out there on the street somewhere and say 'I've got one' and you'll get mobbed being hired—right now, because of the push."

Shifting patterns of fashion and availability place a premium on the employment of certain categories of workers. Minority women and men, professionals and nonprofessionals alike, know the burdens of hiring under the auspices of "affirmative action." Generally, however, workers of the "wrong" sex seem to have been more easily accepted here than have those of the wrong color, though this acceptance varies with time and place. The Northwest is ethnically homogeneous, although there are limited concentrations of urban minorities. Women of color are still very rare on Forest Service rosters, most especially in field-going positions. The relative scarcity of potential workers of color encourages the employment of white women, while at the same time cheapening their value as affirmative action targets. When compared with minority men, women were originally seen as both more accessible and less threatening. One of the first women hired recalls: "When there were women to hire, you didn't have to hire blacks or Chicanos, because they could get their minorities—that's why we were called [his] 'niggers' and showpieces, OK? Because he had filled his quota of minorities with women and didn't have any blacks or Chicanos."

No consensus exists on the relative prospects of majority women and minority men and women, although some male managers and workers suspect a preference for male companionship and leadership. More importantly, the regional ethnic distribution will continue to mean greater representation of majority women. Many see discrimination based on race or physical handicap as the appropriate target of affirmative action now. As one particularly sanguine woman put it: "If you do them a good job, it don't matter if you wear a bra or jockey shorts. . . . It just doesn't seem to matter anymore." But a few managers indicate that they would hire an ethnic male over a female applicant at present, sensing a renewed emphasis on ethnic access. Some also predict administrative positions will come more easily to the ethnic than to the sexual minority. Minority women are nearly universally overlooked in these speculations about the future.

For those minority workers (however defined) who did succeed in joining, a number of formal organizational channels now exist for defining and airing problems. Career counseling for women is available in some districts, and most units in these two study areas have designated equal employment opportunity counselors whose job is to attempt informal resolution of problems and, failing that, to facilitate the formal complaint process. At the national forest level, a Civil Rights Advisory Committee (CRAC) meets regularly with delegates from all units to monitor progress and to advise the forest supervisor. Each national forest in turn is represented on the regional Civil Rights Action Group (CRAG). In addition, both study forests employ equal employment opportunity specialists at the personnel level, and most units have local representatives in the National Federation of Federal Employees (NFFE). Regardless of wide variation in the atmosphere in which these groups operate, this extensive machinery for voicing and analyzing problems is significant.

Formal training sessions of various kinds are held regularly by the Forest Service, and these now address such topics as women and management, with human rights sessions designed to raise consciousness and to secure the commitment of supervisors to the principles of equal opportunity for all workers. While they vary widely in quality (and one man at the end of the session he attended on human rights blandly noted, "I'd have killed every damn one of you"), they can facilitate informal and frank discussion of sexism and racism, stereotyping and discrimination.

Some of the national forests also participate in programs designed to recruit and retain minority workers through cooperative education programs combining college study and periods of employment culminating in guaranteed permanent work. Relatively few minority workers find jobs this way (and some charge that such programs are used more by white males), but the approach has been successful for some.

Both study forests also participate in the Federal Women's Program (FWP), which allots time (15 percent) to one woman in the supervisor's office to coordinate the program and time also (5 percent) for unit-level FWP representatives to encourage grass-roots activity. The program takes different forms and is fundamentally shaped by the personalities of those actively involved and by the local problems and management. Some activities have included career planning seminars, access to classes in women's studies and assertiveness training, attitudinal surveys and monthly newsletters, lectures and informal lunches. It was one of the early vehicles for the informal organization of women, and its formal recognition resulted from the struggles of feminist women in the organization.

Management lends formal support to affirmative action, and the "party line" is not difficult to hear, although it is less uniform than we might expect. Those units next door to the supervisor's or regional offices appear especially eager to please; in an organization so sensitive to public relations, this public visibility is important. More isolated units gain a limited autonomy, with slack for evasion of policy in this and other ways.

The atmosphere in which women begin their work is constantly and subtly shifting. One manager's change of heart is illustrative. After coming to terms with his own prejudices and the need to rectify what he sees as the methodical exclusion of women and minorities, he now reports a lost faith in affirmative action. Reduced to a "body count" and ploy to "run the flag up," the program no longer attracts his interest or concern. The trend to integration takes on a new and disturbing character: "After a while, in my view, that got to be sort of an insatiable appetite. . . . It was almost as though that was a right they now enjoyed, and that right was going to be pushed forever."

The turn away from affirmative action worries supporters of a more open organization. In the face of apparent opportunity but limited progress, women and minorities must continue to "stay on top of those people, to keep people straight." Many feel a "continuous battle" must be waged in many different ways and places. And it is only more difficult to wage in a new national climate of retrenchment and antagonism to governmental affirmative action programs. The most concerned individuals worry about organizational indifference and the single-minded pursuit of personal careers: "The struggle for equality goes on and on and on. Actually, we're really backsliding. . . . It's women who make me mad, because they could do so much more for themselves."

Districts develop traditions and reputations—some are notoriously difficult for women, others by comparison are oases of opportunity and sensitivity. The support of key people is greater than all the organizational machinery together, making the difference between a CRAC existing only on paper and one that is engaged in meaningful dialogue with administrators, or between an activist FWP and one given only bemused lip service. The sentiments of a unit manager and his top supervisors can have great impact. This fact is clear when one unit loses—and another gains—a manager opposed to an active FWP, to mixed-sex work pairs, to women workers on brush disposal crews (BD crews), or to cohabitation without marriage in government housing.

The strength and potential of affirmative action in the Forest Service is controversial. Some bitterly pronounce it "a joke—good on paper, but it isn't really happening," and others imagine "lady rangers" are just around the corner. Then there are the disbelievers, who bide their time until women return to women's work. Like the young man who cynically tolerates demands for sexual "mingling" on field crews (which soon "wear off" anyway), they await the return of less complicated days. Should dire predictions be fulfilled, they reserve escape routes; one plans a retreat to logging, where he "won't have to be nice to anybody." To some the issue is simple: "If you live and work in the United States you have a right to work where you want to work—it's just as simple as that," one man pronounces. Others agree with the manager who objects only to certain kinds of women: "If you want to get into a nontraditional role and you want to be a real activist about it, I'd get into a different organization. . . . You won't fit in well with the Forest Service with that attitude."

At lower levels, where more women are hired and hence work more with men, the principles and programs of affirmative action are openly more controversial. Top-down emphasis on good faith efforts to meet hiring goals smacks of coercion to some, and hostility toward the central administrative offices is easily galvanized by allusion to this topic. The feeling is widespread that the local affirmative action "report card" (quarterly reports on hiring) reflects on the general reputation of the unit and its chief administrators particularly. If heads do not exactly roll when progress is judged inadequate, the carrot is definitely in evidence: awards are made to individuals and units honoring notable efforts and results, and managers proudly display them.

The policy of affirmative action in hiring can be kinder to men's careers than to women; the activist man is liberal and has credentials, while the activist woman is often simply overworked. Ambitious men are often frank about their self-interested conversion to the cause and about the positive impact of this reputation and the visibility it affords them. Even the most forgiving of women are ambivalent about the possibility that a powerful man will see them as a "star in his crown." A professional woman describes her boss with mixed feelings: "He didn't like me because I called him on his professional judgment, but he did like me for being a woman working under him, and it made him look good. He's very supportive of women, because it looks very good in the Forest Service in this day and age to do this, to give this lip service."

In a sense, there are top-down and bottom-up versions of affirmative action and the position and future of women field workers. There are almost two organizational histories, somewhat at odds—the one formal and official, the other underground, unrecorded, a kind of subterranean oral history of struggle. It is handed down by old-timers, those who were the shock troops of change and bear the battle scars. Their story is not always well known or credited by the younger women entering the woods five and ten years later, nor is the feminist movement always recognized for its inspiration and support of insurgency. Other women do recognize this organizational and social history and fully acknowledge its contribution to the atmosphere in which field-going women work.

As more women are hired for field jobs, the potential for support grows, although a feminist or activist reputation in the Forest Service can be a burden. If the male majority—"just the *mass* of them"—discourages women in male-dominated workplaces, progress toward a critical mass of women field workers can only help. One woman remembers her first field job in a particularly hostile district: "We faced it together. . . . I don't know if I could have faced it alone. I probably could have if I'd had to, but it was real nice having another woman."

Women field workers committed to securing an equitable future will make the difference between a meaningful and a purely symbolic and divisive affirmative action program. The interviews convey an emerging conviction that feminist spirit and organization can be powerful—and that the time has come. Significantly, some of those who "cut [more] slack" than they wished to out of concern for their careers now feel secure enough to risk more: "I think that's where we really do have to be stronger. And some of us have got to . . . , got to start the fight and maybe do a little sacrificing to change it."

Beginning Woods Work

Field workers in similar situations—whether "ground stompers" in the Northwest or Southwest, male or female—share similarities of job attitude and behavior. Thus there are many parallels in the experiences of female and male temporaries, as in the world views of high-status professional men and women in the Forest Service as well. Yet being a woman in a sexist society shapes women's lives before and after beginning work each morning. Critical differences in typical styles, likely futures, job behaviors and attitudes, self-definition and commitment, are rooted outside the workplace and extend into lives beyond work. These differences may become more apparent when women enter the male domain of woods work.

These pioneering women begin their work with different feelings and expectations. It is often a difficult decision to take the plunge and risk entering a radically different kind of workplace. Sheer ignorance of the future makes the process easier for some. Looking back, the tree-climbing cone picker remembers when she thought her new job would probably mean "standing in a ticket booth or something—I had no idea—playground superintendent maybe!" The night before reporting to their new jobs, many women spent anxious hours wondering why the opportunity had once seemed a good idea and worrying about what might happen to them. They wondered about the work and their ability to measure up, about how boyfriends, husbands, and family really felt, and about the expectations or demands of the men at work.

Some few knew long summers spent building fence or baling hay, but most had no such background to lend perspective to their new work. Those who were experienced with demanding manual labor jobs, in the local mills or on family farms, or who were high school athletic stars or cross-country skiers, entered with more confidence.[10] But even the experienced backpacker soon learned that there is all the difference in the world between playing and working in the woods, between leisurely hiking and carrying forty-pound "bladder bags" of water up hills to lightning strikes in the dead heat of summer. Many of the experienced and the inexperienced, the athletes and the heavy smokers, were a jumble of nerves, self-doubt, and contradictory emotions about tackling the new job. Warnings from friends and families—often lovers and husbands—about the extreme physical demands in store (especially, but not exclusively, in fire control) added to last-minute anxieties. Sometimes, too, there were subtle warnings of "lost femininity" in store, and the future seemed altogether too much, too risky.

Some women brought to their new job extraordinary self-confidence ("I don't think there is anything in the world I can't learn to do") and all were eager to give it a try, though they had a lot to learn. "Tomboys" though they had been, the vast majority were reared in families honoring traditional patterns of the sexual division of labor.[11] They might have helped in the garage and yard, but they were permanently on call around the kitchen as well. Their concrete skills from a boy's world were few. The middle-aged rancher to whom "everything just came naturally" when he switched to forestry and the young woman from Cleveland, reared to love the outdoors but not to put chains on a pickup truck, are simply two extremes of difference. This early training and typical lack of physical work follow them years later into the workplace.

Forestry work is especially inviting. The opportunity is still rare for women to develop their bodies fully. To work outside and to work hard and to work with men—all these were attractions of the new job not often shared by male co-workers. Women knew far too well the boredom and isolation of the steno pool and the aches and anxieties of the waitress. One thirty-year-old field worker, for example, had already worked as a seasonal airline stewardess, phone company representative, ski instructor, customer representative, city clerk, traffic engineer, cashier, waitress, barmaid, and computer programmer. Others had not had this same breadth of experience but shared the relentless search for "work I didn't actually *hate*."

In the small towns dominated by the Forest Service and perhaps a lumber mill, government work at government wages is attractive, particularly now that a woman's options there are not limited to the clerical series. She is considered today for jobs involving clearing trails, "stacking sticks," water monitoring, supervising tree-planting crews, trapping mountain beaver, and (perhaps more reluctantly) fire fighting. "Slashing beats hashing," as one old-timer put it, and the chance for different work at decent wages is attractive to many women. The jobs may be odd and the conditions unusual, but women are happy to have them—both in 1968 ("Listen here, you bald-headed pup—for $2.30 an hour I can drop my drawers behind *any* tree!") and in 1978 ("Don't get too upset about the things you're going to be assigned to do, because for that $4.20 an hour, you can do weird stuff!").

This group of new workers was thrilled (even if also uncertain and uneasy) to be starting their new jobs. Learning new skills and meeting new challenges is especially valued by those accustomed to the routine tasks of service, clerical, and sales jobs. And the opportunity to experience "that *good* tired feeling" was appreciated even as they struggled with gloves and pants too big by far, with back-breaking tree planting on alarmingly steep hillsides, and with enough slush and mud, smoke and heat, to leave a person forever exhausted and filthy.

All this means more to some than to others, and those just beginning to work bring a different perspective from that of workers with years of experience in and out of the household. So too the opportunity to learn surveying or timber cruising means something different to "the type of woman who changes her own tires" or who is "right out of the house—doesn't know zilch." For those with years in low-paying dead-end jobs, the Forest Service careers they now enjoy have transformed their lives in delightful and unexpected ways. More than one takes real pride in her growth and values equally her new economic independence and self-confidence:

> It's really been quite an experience. I led more or less a very sheltered life, and the Forest Service has made me realize that . . . my opinion meant

something. You know, they listen to me, they make me feel good. Well, my first husband told me one time that I wasn't smart enough to do anything that anybody would be willing to pay me for! I've been working ever since he said that. I really feel good about it.

Overall, the women share a feeling of good fortune and a common determination to do well and make good the opportunity for themselves and for other women in the future.

Also distinguishing the new women workers from the men they work with is the profound influence of family. Few of this group could or would have come to work in the woods without the support (or occasionally benign neglect) of their families—children, husbands, and parents. Many parents are initially disturbed by the disparity between their daughters' work and the lives they had envisioned for their offspring, though often criticism slowly turned to acceptance and even to pride, particularly among fathers. The growing recognition of women in non-traditional jobs has brought more than one parent or husband around: "Dad's so proud of me he just bubbles. He just *loves* to tell people what I do. He thinks it's so neat that his daughter's not the typical secretary."

Fathers who were themselves farmers or loggers find the occupation easier to accept, though they also worry about their daughters' choice of a lifelong career of physical labor, and fathers tend to worry too about the unbalanced sex ratio. Knowing best what such a male-dominated atmosphere can be, they would wish her well away. Some families worry about the danger—of being gobbled by bears or lost forever in the deep forest—more than about the more likely back injury. Still, in a time of high unemployment a job of any kind pleases, and government work seems to offer a certain security and responsibility, especially to daughters as yet unmarried.

Some families understand better than others, and some approve largely out of ignorance. Daughters and wives may fabricate or camouflage details—regarding out-of-town training sessions with three men, for instance, or solitary traverses in the woods during lunch, or working the fire line at a forest fire. Work for the Forest Service is sometimes a family affair, though, with spouse and sons-in-law and now daughters too employed in some capacity for Smokey. And the many Forest Service couples often trace the roots of their affection to work on the same crew, to shared office space, or to a particular training session or project fire.

Women's family responsibilities and living situations profoundly affect career patterns, from preferred hours and conditions to job attitude and ambition. One temporary worker welcomes seasonal work because it allows her the winter season to "get my house back in order again," while another cannot afford to continue seasonal employment, for to her surprise she is still self-supporting: "It never occurred to me I was going to have to work for a living most of my life. I just *assumed* that I was of course going to get married like everybody else does—don't they?!"

For women with families, their help is essential if she is to pursue training or to attend lucrative project fires likely to take her suddenly hundreds of miles from home for uncertain periods of time. She will be the one to arrange for child care, and if it is unavailable, she will not work; she will likely leave her job when her husband leaves his. Without an unusual degree of cooperation at home, she limits her job and future. Only a few of the younger generation of field-working women have yet come face-to-face with this situation: "It just doesn't go. . . . It's asking too much to have my husband have to take care of family for a whole week while I'm gone."

Relations with men at home shape relations with men at work, just as career development for women is structured in part by family and marital status. The married woman may not join her co-workers at the tavern but may hurry home to start dinner or may opt out of skinny-dipping in the back woods to honor delicate male feelings of propriety. The single woman, on the other hand, may engage wholeheartedly in the district's social life and in the activities of the Forest Service "family," with very different consequences for her work life. For women, family and love life and work world are never discrete or inviolate but rather jointly determine the nature of her days in the kitchen, bedroom, and work-place. This state of affairs is regarded as normal for the employed woman (and is too often ignored for working men), and it represents the shared context for working women who are otherwise very different.

In these and other ways, then, the experiences of field-going women are incomparable, and their situation vastly differs from that of the men beside whom they will work during the summer and years to come. Some feel the difference more than others, but as a group they shared the eagerness and the secret worries of the night before as they prepared to launch new jobs, to meet new people, to work in new ways. They are the changers and the changed. What will happen to them? What will they find, and what will their own impact be?

Summary

This study has a particular organizational, political, and historical context. The entry of women into field work takes place within a powerful federal agency in which both policy and activity are highly visible to the public. Women's entry into formerly all-male enclaves in this highly stratified organization began some years ago and yet remains problematic. The period is one of high unemployment and raging inflation, with a corresponding shift to the right politically, symbolized by restrictions on the taking and spending of public monies as well as organized opposition to "social issues" touching directly on the status of women, from abortion to the Equal Rights Amendment.

The women and men personally involved in the politics of affirmative action are a diverse group, though they share a common affinity for outdoor work and leisure and often a similar class and cultural background as well. At the same time, there are important and systematic differences in the perspective women and men bring to bear on their work, particularly as women learn nontraditional forestry skills.

Those who speak here are not representative samples of larger populations, but instead represent the major work situations and styles of the organization. Through their particularity, their single voices and shared concerns, we glimpse the outlines of social change as women and men come together in the woods and the office, along the trails, and at the potlucks of these two national forests of the Northwest.

3

Early Challenges
and Opportunities

Women become field workers in the Forest Service in a number of ways and for many different reasons. While each story is unique, several ways of "coming on board" predominate. None of the group pursued forestry work from ideological commitment to nontraditional work. Few, indeed, had much idea how very male dominated their new occupation was. Only a handful planned and pursued professional careers in forestry that brought them into Forest Service work; women with forestry degrees have a broad range of options, and the Forest Service is not always at the top of the list. Whether or not they had college degrees, most of these workers looked to the Forest Service either because it is the major local employer in their area and they must work, or because it is a way of supporting a preferred life-style in a chosen area (e.g., upriver or on the coast).

Whatever the motivation, these woods-working women count themselves lucky, often remarking the "accidental" twists and turns of life and career choices. One young temporary worker, now happily returning as a regular "temporary" slash piler, says she "just lucked out." She had recently moved with her husband to the small town in the Oregon woods and was tiring of her job pumping gas when a male friend visited and used their telephone for messages. When the Forest Service called him about his application she took advantage of the moment and asked "if they had any other opening, for women." She was fortunate enough to speak with a clerk who advised her that women too were hired on brush disposal crews to clear popular scenic roadways of unsightly slash from logging. She happily applied and went to work: "I liked outdoor work, and I couldn't see anything besides working down at the A & W, and I can't handle that."

Five years earlier the climate was much different. It took the first women field workers two years to get their jobs. The annual tree-planting festival held locally by the community convinced a group of older housewives that they too could plant trees. One of these path-breaking women remembers: "We decided if little kids and old men could do it, there's no reason why we couldn't do it." She and the others went to work getting jobs from the local district as tree planters: "We just started dingin' them, and they wouldn't give us a job because there were no comfort stations in the woods, besides, women wouldn't work out. How do you know? Because they're just not capable, blah, blah, blah. They just can't do it. The terrain's too rough, the weather's too bad."

Eventually these women prevailed, won the chance they asked for, and proved themselves responsible and competent beyond anyone's expectation. Never forgetting their original reception, still they count themselves well treated and generally well received. Laughingly they recall how they were assumed incompetent, were given especially rugged tasks, and were shepherded about by a young man assigned to watch over the "lady tree planters"—and were given whistles to help them take discreet bathroom breaks away from his eyes. Today they tell the tale with the good humor and forbearance of the loyal opposition. For these old-timers, whose careers in field work predate affirmative action plans and the feminist movement, the entry of other women into outdoor jobs today seems to proceed with great ease, perhaps too easily.

One group of women woods workers enters through clerical work. Field jobs may come unexpectedly, as to the recently divorced clerk applying for temporary work, who soon found herself reassigned to the regional fire-fighting crew. Another worked indoors until her appointment ended, when the only other opening in the area made her eventually the Northwest's first female road inspector. A few women sought clerical jobs deliberately, seeing them as the best route to permanent employment in the federal system, from which they hoped to maneuver into work in another series. Some did just this, watching and learning, planning their move into the technical series at the first opportunity. Other secretaries had no such intention, but watching the men go off to the woods every day finally became too much: "Sometimes they spend an hour driving before they even get to their job. And you know, that's what we used to do for *treats,* was to go out in the woods for a ride! So right away I figured I had to get outside. Well, it took me about three years to really get out."

Familiarity with the paperwork of a job can make a woman the most qualified person to fill a slot. Gradual promotions may take her into work previously performed only by men (though involving clerical work) and thus into the technical series. This progression does not always occur. In one case a GS-7 job in the technical series was redefined as a GS-5 in the clerical series when women began to qualify, in effect downgrading the position to correspond with the sexual status of the typical worker.

Several women in the sample were placed after completing Job Corps training in the area; others came as students. At the four-year college level, a few women enter as cooperative education students, integrating academic study with regular periods of employment in the Forest Service, culminating (with satisfactory performance and academic work) in a guaranteed permanent job.

Students in forestry traditionally work summers in field jobs, and college students in other fields also apply successfully. Both two- and four-year forestry degree programs require field experience. Professors generally help their students find jobs—and are sometimes accused of sexual bias as they do so. Local women enrolled in forest technician programs have attempted a lawsuit over the issue in the past. Faculty are accused (though not universally) of slighting women, discouraging their interest and learning, and generally making them feel uncomfortable and unwanted. Female students in various forestry programs report "sexy" entries in classroom slide shows, flirtatious faculty, the occasional hostile male student, and deans determined to keep women from joining overnight field trips. Still, they generally report a fairly positive reception from other students, especially when no direct cooperation or competition is involved and when the work is academic and indoors.

Recognizing the limited mobility of most low-level workers, the Forest Service participates in a federal job program designed to facilitate the upward mobility of workers, particularly by moving women out of the clerical series. The upward mobility jobs have helped a number of this group to move into nontraditional jobs. Promising women interested in new work compete for training positions enabling them to move up gradually and without direct competition. With guaranteed training and promotion, they become skilled inspectors or computer specialists or surveyors, able to compete successfully for higher-level positions.

Some women object that this mobility is fairly limited, generally topping at the GS-5 level, while the clerical series tops at a GS-4, and that the training integral to the program does not always materialize. While men can and do take upward mobility jobs, the program is designed for women in dead-end positions, primarily clerical. Some indoor women feel a natural resentment that their only hope for promotion lies in working outside with men, doing men's jobs.

Supervisors can promote for failure in this program. A disgruntled field worker complains that in her department the first upward mobility candidate was a very young, cute, and male-identified woman fearful of snakes and dirt: "They know what they've got. . . . they're not stupid."

The match of job and worker readily confirms stereotypes about women and work. A manager casually comments on the way in which he identifies potential upward mobility job categories: "OK, here's a position a woman could do really well at." Some upward mobility jobs serve to preserve rigorous work for "people who should be out in the brush" by involving the redesign of positions to separate clerical and field tasks. The required field work in the timber sale appraisal position, for instance, is flexible. Expectations are easily "toned down a little bit" to accommodate a woman in the job, thus "freeing" men from the more clerical aspects of contract work.

By no means a panacea for clerical women, for some the upward mobility program provides a transition from one line of work to another, with the necessary support, training, and temporary freedom from competition. Upward mobility slots can become jumping-off points for women eager to move on or can as easily become in time new low-level "women's jobs" within the technical series.

"Politicking" and judicious use of the influence of key insiders play pivotal roles in some women's hiring, most especially in the case of rehires and transfers but also including first hires for those (few) women who are savvy enough to pursue actively the personal touch in hiring. Sheer persistence (repeatedly calling or "camping out on their front doorstep") paid off for other determined applicants. Grapevine knowledge of districts and national forests open to women is also very helpful.

The agency not long ago converted to a national computerized system of hiring. This step took summer jobs out of the hands of local districts, where they had occasionally been used in "pork barrel" style, and promised objectivity in employment. There is a widespread feeling on the part of management and employees close to it that this measure has effectively eliminated sexual bias in hiring, and an equally strong sentiment to the contrary among individuals lower down who still feel the power of the personal appeal. Particularly in the case of transfers and rehires, managers will seek information about job applicants. As one district ranger confided: "All the merit business aside, it requires you to know people. And when somebody's being considered for a job, the telephone still rings—'Hey, what do you know about old Harry, or old Jake?'"

At the annual "slave market," during which temporaries are hired out to districts from central hiring lists, there is a certain amount of dickering and bartering as districts bargain for favorite workers and pawn off less satisfactory workers elsewhere. Physical appearance can be a factor in hiring, computers notwithstanding. On one unit, the manager is notorious for his insistence upon good-looking young women in front desk jobs and personally hires only women who meet his standards; thus "he's got some of the damndest ding-a-lings you ever saw."

One woman remembers her disillusionment when a very reliable source told her that her boss, renowned for his support of women, had engineered the hiring of an attractive woman to work with his friend, widely known to prefer only attractive female co-workers. Another bitterly relates the running joke of the department: why not hire the local barmaid if the office really needs a draftsman? No woman in this study felt that her own job rested solely upon her appearance—but some wondered, when promotion brought rumor and gossip.

However they find their way into field work, most women woods workers enter with temporary appointments only. Of the permanent women in this group, more than a third worked first as temporaries; many worked for years as seasonals, especially in the tree and seed nurseries, where temporary part-time work is the rule. Working as a temporary is the easiest way to secure a permanent job. Without the experience and references it provides (and in the absence of professional credentials), permanent jobs are extremely difficult to win.

Temporary and permanent employees enjoy decidedly different organizational positions in terms of responsibility, reputation, benefits, worries, futures, and social circles. Not all temporaries jump at the chance to apply for permanent positions, preferring regular part-time work with unemployment benefits or winter employment and the opportunity to travel, study, or simply relax during the off season. Some are still floating, looking for a satisfying way of life, while others use part-time field work to support other interests.

Still, most seasonal workers who enjoy their work and are not in school do seek permanent work. Temporaries tire of their reputation as lazy, irresponsible workers, motivated only by economic pressure to take low-paying, difficult jobs. They may seek more "input into the system" as permanents, or the security of full-time employment, or more interesting work unavailable to temporaries. As permanent slots become scarce, female candidates must have exceptional determination and qualifications. Managers are reluctant to risk placing untried workers in scarce job slots, and female newcomers especially.

The ranger quoted below illustrates the diversity of opinion in his area on the question of gambling with a female field worker:

Some people say "Hey, OK, if I hire a woman I may wind up having some of these problems, you know, with the wives and all that. But I'm willing to accept that because I think women are going to be able to do the job just as good as men." There's other guys that say, "Hey, why take on a hassle? Maybe they can, maybe they can't do the job, but we're getting along just fine without them, why take them—and I'm not going to get paid any more, so why have another hassle?" And then you have the other person who says, "I really think this is a need, that I feel—you know, in terms of the nation's need—and I want to do something personally."

Women and men alike complain of obscure procedures, unpredictable roster openings, low ratings by the Civil Service Commission, and "wired" jobs rigged in advance for an inside candidate. Women complain too of rosters top-heavy with veterans, who effectively deprive them of a chance to compete for some positions. Several have deliberately downgraded temporarily in order to circumvent the veteran bottleneck blocking the way on the appropriate roster. Temporary women must often downgrade temporarily (e.g., from a GS-4 position to a GS-3) in order to win a permanent job.

Friendships and run-ins, successes and shortcomings, all follow temporaries as they move about this very mobile organization. One woman objected when her boss hesitated to use women field workers in certain jobs, earning her the reputation (in her words) of "rebel rouser." Recognizing this burden and her supervisor's power, she did not attempt to apply for a permanent job at that district. Even so, the permanent job she was eventually given was contingent upon an implied promise exacted by her new supervisor that she would not continue this behavior, which had been reported to him firsthand just as unsatisfactory job performance would have been.

Influential friends can help too. Some districts will work the rule book as effectively as they can to find a good job for a woman they want to keep; others wait until the woman with six years in as a temporary threatens to quit before they take her seriously. There is a general sense that things are always possible, and women recall fondly the personnel clerks and secretaries, former rangers, and bosses who put in the word for them. A manager seconds this feeling: "I felt OK about what we were doing. We were bending a lot of rules to hire minorities. And I felt all right about that, because we had bent a lot of rules to hire Joe down the road, and so I didn't see any difference. . . . And we had methodically kept people from having opportunities."

However they enter their new jobs, field-going women go to work in a highly charged atmosphere, as token women in previously male domains. One of the first challenges they face is sexual stereotyping in job placement and crew relations.

The Sexual Division of Labor

Women field workers in the Forest Service do work in almost every outdoor job—somewhere, to some degree, at some time. Yet stereotypic ideas about women have a very real impact on how women enter the organization, from the department into which they are hired to the daily informal division of labor, from the morning drive to the afternoon report.

One dimension of sex segregation is job placement through the internal labor market. Women field workers tend to be concentrated in certain aspects of field work. Although there are a few women rappellers, geologists, and dispatchers, most field workers cluster in the major departments of fire control, timber management, engineering, and recreation. Within departments, the women in this study are found more often in fairly predictable places: in fire control, they work most often on the slash-piling crews and only rarely join tanker crews or suppression crews; in survey, women will more often clear brush along survey lines than run the survey instruments; in timber, women tend to mark timber sale boundaries rather than manage timber sales.[1]

Yet in this occupation, the boundaries are fluid. Districts vary widely in placing field-going women. Women in one district, for example, are amazed to hear that others not far away work regularly with men on the brush disposal crews so carefully limited to men on their home turf. Similarly, women who carry fuel-dripping torches to light slash-burn fires, a fairly dangerous but prestigious and exciting task, enjoy a job limited in some places largely to men but routinely rotated elsewhere. Driving water-pumping trucks, which demands experience and confidence with cumbersome, dual-axle, and very expensive vehicles, is another example of this variation. In some districts "that's *all* they let her do," while elsewhere women are still fighting for the chance to try. Women "firsts" working on the sophisticated regional computer system of timber resources (Timber Resource Inventory, or TRI) are elsewhere fairly routine.

Barriers are pushed farther, sooner, and more effectively in certain times and places, reflecting the strength of local tradition and prejudice, women field workers' experience and desire, and labor demands.[2] Managers with low-level openings may risk trying women in unconventional jobs more readily than will those with only GS-7 or GS-9 openings. When three new timber sale officers are hired, experimental placement of a woman is more likely than when a district employs only one officer.

There is often considerable variety in field work, as much of it is cyclical, or project work, or all too contingent upon weather conditions, creating opportunities for temporary training and experience in other fields. When pressure rises in one department (e.g., to pick the cones of those parent trees selected as superior tree stock in reforestation efforts), all available help may be detailed to fill in, giving women exposure to different kinds of work and broadening their circles of acquaintance. During fire season, fighting fires takes first priority, and all workers can be asked to help out in some capacity. When women transfer around the districts and national forests (especially the mobile temporaries), they are very often hired into the department with the greatest need.

Traditional patterns may be situational, as when a pregnant worker is assigned lighter duty temporarily. All-women crews sometimes occur by force of circumstance rather than by design, though the policy of pairing the experienced and the inexperienced usually separates women. When circumstances demand the most skilled workers—to organize a crew effectively under pressure or to complete a rush job—the luxury of sexual bias is apt to be abandoned quickly: "Fire is a perfect example. They'll send the women to do something safe, like go get some hoses, and they'll send men down where the fire is crowning out. . . . But when things are really coming down, when the fire's really going, I think that stuff gets forgotten real quick, and the job just gets done. It's just whoever's there."

Decisions concerning the distribution of work are made by supervisors and crews in many different ways—from considering the sheer size of the crew reporting to work on a dreary Monday to accommodating the "Incredible Hulk" who so enjoys using the chain saw. Tasks considered important, for instance, will always be reserved for those most skilled. When productivity is important, workers' relative skill, strength, and physical condition will all take priority in job assignments. Sloppy writers, male or female, will not take survey notes, and bad backs keep women and men alike from lifting heavy bags of fertilizer. Seniority is also a factor, especially in distributing the unpopular "shit work." Sometimes distasteful or unpopular tasks—trapping the mountain beaver which damages seedlings, or striping the new logging roads with paint—are routinely rotated. More skilled and prestigious tasks are not always so freely shared.

Some work is assigned to women for essentially punitive reasons. The early all-woman tree-planting crews were often given "dirty work"—the steepest hillsides in the area to plant, for instance. A woman overheard her supervisor threaten to "work her until her titties hang down to her knees." One fire management officer (FMO) was reported to have successfully kept women off his fire suppression crews by instituting instead apparently progressive all-woman brush disposal crews. Sex-segregated work crews can also serve as a diversionary tactic, as when two women assigned to a pumper truck were sent off repeatedly without a radio, "polishing the fire truck," in effect, for they could not be called in a fire emergency.

Underlying these shifting patterns in the sexual division of labor is the murkier terrain of preference, affect, and personal relationship. The key question becomes not which particular jobs women tend to perform, but what the significance and consequence are. There seem always to be deeper dimensions of segregation and containment, keeping alive at some level the fundamentally distinct relations of women and men to each other and to their work. The concept of division of labor broadens to include who does what parts of a task and who insists on prerogative, how decisions are made, how specialties emerge, and how judgments are passed. The arena includes the coffee room, the pickup, and the office.

The impulse to draw on sexual distinctions is always manifest. On one crew, driving up logging roads to the job site may be monopolized by men, while elsewhere men happily share that burden but opt out of tasks taking them near paper or typewriters. The "nicer" trashcans (less heavy or foul) will be given to women to empty, and when chains must be put on, women are often not expected or encouraged to help.

During slack times, women field workers may work in the office while their partners do carpentry work out back. A woman will be assigned to reorganize the filing system during bad weather, a task long postponed when only men were available. Drafting and typing tasks may come to her in a pinch too. Explaining why clerical tasks fall more often to her, one woman remarks unselfconsciously, "I'm the only one there"—the only woman, that is, among the immediate group.

Traditional patterns in gender relations represent themselves as efficient, reasonable, and benign. Indeed, the sexual division of labor may contribute to reducing uncertainties at work, as in the following case. On a survey crew of long standing, several excellent partnerships developed among returning workers. All those contacted adamantly asserted that their work was shared equally, structured only by the intrinsic demands of the labor, the number of bodies available on a given day, and natural inclination. Later, describing the pleasure she took in her partnership, one of these women inadvertently confirmed the ubiquity of sex-based patterns in the division of labor, at whatever level:

> Like, [he] would do the brushing, he'd take over the chain saw, getting the equipment, making sure it was working right, and if it needed to be fixed, fixing the equipment and making sure the rig was running right. I'd take over the notes and the people, say who's going to do what work and who's

going to go where. And it worked out really good, because we really worked *with* each other. We just really clicked.

Women confront a multiplicity of beliefs about women generally and in forest work particularly. The manager may feel that because women excelled in high school, they will be good professional foresters as well, able "to deal in a more mature manner with the paperwork than the brush-beating man." They may seem excellent workers in campground maintenance, for "it may have been that they were more tidy with their own life, their home life, and so it carried over on to the job." Women may seem the perfect candidates for fire lookouts, a job demanding patience, attention to detail, diligence, and curiosity. Men may find a woman more natural in reforestation work, where supervisors report her more "meticulous" and honest in doing boring work. So too managers may hear from fire control bosses that women excel with "people and paper" (i.e., on prevention patrol or dispatch) but not in digging fire lines. As tree planters they may "pretty it up" and be "more conscious of doing a good job, whereas the guys are more conscious of making money."

The traditional division of labor is seen to accommodate the presumed physical disabilities of women and at the same time to maximize compensatory presumed strengths. This is so regardless of the details of the argument or job assignment in question, for the beauty of the rationale is that it always fits. Women can be superior tree planters because they are more conscientious, particularly regarding "baby trees," and at the same time they can be said to be inferior at the back-breaking labor of tree planting. The key theme is functional efficiency based on complementary partnerships of natural strength. Thus some men gladly welcome women into their terrain because they are able to assume some of the more routine bureaucratic tasks while "freeing" men for their true vocation in the woods. And some women are very happy to do so for just that reason.

On field crews, each job is often different, if only slightly, from all others, and may involve sets of clearly defined roles (e.g., the head and rear chainman in survey). In those cases where all tasks are rotated and jobs more nearly identical (e.g., slash piling or fire suppression), the major remaining arena for the cultivation of sexual difference and display of ability and inability is the matter of physical strength—and it rarely fails to appear. Men throughout the organization voluntarily take the steeper or more rugged terrain to work, split a heavy load unequally, and slow the pace of their work and walk when around women.

Assumptions about sexual strengths and weaknesses are rooted in the home and culture but become powerful forces at work, justifying and facilitating traditional relations there and confirming the status quo even in the face of the direct challenge represented by women in the woods. There is always room at some level to accommodate these convictions, and sometimes too there is occasion to challenge them. Women feel very differently about this subject. Some outdo even the most conservative managers in arguing for natural differences and take real satisfaction in every opportunity to compensate with more feminine skills for shortcomings as woods workers. Others fight every manifestation of a sex-based division of labor, whether it is being assigned to a timekeeper role at fire camp (and refusing it), being assumed responsible for the empty coffee pot (and pointedly teaching others how to make coffee), or being given the lighter tasks and the easy way out (and steadfastly climbing out of the truck to help anyway with the flat tire).

There is room for both types of women and all those in between in the organization, although for the challenging women things will never come easily. It is always simpler to take advantage of traditional assumptions, to accept help graciously, to defer to superior strength—to go along rather than to risk the reputation of the "libber" or the "macho woman." Further, the path-breaker role is not always compatible with personal interest and inclination. While keenly aware of the scarcity of women in timber, especially at the higher levels, one woman reluctantly acknowledges her own preference for reforestation work instead, while detesting the identification of reforestation as a field "good for women": "But it's *us* as much as anything. I'd just as soon get out of timber. . . . I mean, I wish I could be that woman—who could go be the dynamite timber sales officer of the century. But it's not within my conscience to do it . . . , and it's not within my interests."

Ambivalence, guilt, and self-doubt are natural companions for those who find themselves reluctantly accepting traditional patterns. Because she does tree planting so rarely in her job, one young woman complains of never developing the strength she needs to keep up with the men: "So I did every other job I could think of besides planting trees all day long, and I did it as hard as I could, just so I wouldn't feel so guilty!"

Acutely aware of the tendency of many women (and men) to opt for the ground job of bagging tree cones rather than climbing high in the swaying tree to collect them, another woman struggles with the contradiction between personal inclination and a sense of obligation to challenge stereotypes:

I found myself actually wanting to be a ground person more than climbing. [Many men were "gung-ho on climbing" although it was very windy, wanting the hazard pay which rewards climbs into particularly tall trees.] And we had been told quite strongly not to climb if you didn't feel like it. And that was one day I felt like—well, here I am, being a female, don't want to climb because of my period. . . . And then when they climbed up and came back down, this one macho guy says, "Oh, it was pretty windy up there. I see why you didn't want to climb!"

Simply getting in—competing successfully for that permanent slot or winning that place on the summer field crew—is not all there is to it. Pressures for conformity to traditional patterns are often as great as the lure of unknown skills and new demands, and field-going women respond very differently to this fundamental contradiction. The status and power of gender continue to shape a woman's daily work relations and experiences just as they influenced where she reported to work in the first place. While barriers of various kinds continue to be successfully challenged and the history of women field workers gradually becomes richer and more diverse, there are critical areas still predominantly segregated and only now in the first stages of change. Supervisory relations are one such arena, as the control over the work process and work of others remains a male prerogative only reluctantly relinquished.

Men Supervising Women

In the Forest Service, women rarely train and direct the work or evaluate the performance of others, especially men. While there have been inroads into this male domain (women have served as crew bosses, contract inspectors, youth group crew leaders, and supervisors of the female work force in the tree nurseries), by and large women and men continue to be supervised by men. At the higher levels there is even less organizational experience with female authority (e.g., women department heads or unit managers).

In any field worker's career there are a number of supervisors at different removes from daily work routines, from the crew boss or his assistant (often simply one of the crew given limited and temporary authority) to the department head or unit manager. While all of these men are important, the greatest influence is exerted by the front-line supervisor—the man or men who, regardless of title or formal authority, in fact control and evaluate women's work. It is with the boss a woman meets in the office each morning before heading out, or who joins her in the pickup for the ride to the job, that she develops the most intimate and delicate relations. Others higher up may be appealed to, circumvented, cultivated, or ignored, but the immediate boss must always be dealt with.

Bosses come and go, as temporary assignments or projects, transfers (his and hers), and internal mobility broaden exposure to various kinds of supervisors. But as a whole, these men are probably the single most decisive factor shaping women's work experience, and women must come to grips with them immediately. While the same is true for men as well, particularly in the lower echelons, the sexual status of male bosses enhances their formal authority over female subordinates, lending the relationship a certain tension, even volatility.[3]

What can a boss do for and to the woman working for him? He provides her with training, evaluates her performance regularly, recommends her for promotions or transfers, and generally determines the way her talents will be put to use and her interests developed. He helps set the tone of her treatment, mediates the complaints and criticisms of others, offers advice, and adjudicates disputes. In the best case, he becomes her mentor or organizational sponsor, carefully nurturing her career development, sharing the insider's view of the unit's political topography and advice on maneuvering through it, and extending to her directly and indirectly his own prestige, authority, and status. In this group, women who are satisfied with their work situation invariably report good experiences with their male supervisors.[4] Good front-line supervision seems to be a condition necessary but not sufficient to successful female integration.

Women describe a good boss in glowing terms. He is first of all a fair man, with essentially similar expectations of all those under him, giving women and men alike the opportunity to succeed and to fail—"and he yells at *me* too." He is personable, someone to whom women can talk easily and freely and regarding more than just the job. He is free with his time, attention, and knowledge, interested not in hoarding but in sharing information and in promoting others rather than in protecting his own turf. He provides the training women need and allows them the autonomy and freedom from oversight that they also need to work independently and to develop confidence. He is responsive to complaints or problems, and women can count on him to back them up if need be. His commitment to women's right to pursue field work is challenged and made real daily. He helps concretely too in finding jobs, giving recommendations, offering suggestions, opening doors of many kinds. Sometimes these excellent working relationships extend beyond the confines of work. Some women report learning from their bosses how to drive a standard transmission or how to tune their cars, or enjoying weekend entertainment together.

On New Year's Eve all the field-going women in one department embraced their supervisor in a gigantic group hug for possessing just these qualities: "Well, first of all he really, really likes women, so that . . . really goes a long way. He's always giving you the benefit of the doubt. He'll give you *any* job he thinks you can handle. He trusts you. . . . He's fair to you. He's just a wonderful man. He's that way with men too. He played sexual games with some of the little nineteen-year-old secretaries, but he never has with me."

These new relationships in the Forest Service are intense and rich, transcending barriers of all kinds as caring friendships between supervisors and their women field workers grow. One woman was struck by her boss's tears when she brought him her news—a permanent job at last, though far away: "It's more than a worker-employer relationship with us. It's close. He's like—well, I can't say he's a father image, but I can turn to him. Like, if I was in jail I'd call [him]! And he is my supporter. He's given me a lot of breaks—I think I deserved them, I can't say that he's given me them unduly." Another woman too counts her boss as family, though a generation separates them:

> Oh, he's fantastic, really fantastic. He's really into seeing me make it, which is really strange—there's nothing in it for him. We get along better than if I had to choose him for a friend. . . . All I have to do is go to [him] with a problem or a question or anything, and he'll bend over backwards to do what he can for me. And he's really good to work with, he's extremely good. . . . And I get along fantastic with his wife and family. We just have a really enjoyable day. We're always razzing each other. We're always giving each other problems, troubles. . . . We don't go two feet without the other one tagging along.

This close association is often interpreted sexually. As the rare but recurring relationships of special closeness develop, suspicions are voiced and a boss may be told to back off—by everybody, from the forest supervisor to the boss's wife. Some men find the context of rumor and innuendo so threatening that working alone with a female partner is something they avoid, let alone encouraging a close personal and professional relationship. It is the assumption of self-interested motivation that so angers this man as he remembers hearing from everyone between the district and the supervisor's office that he should see less of the woman he has taken under his wing: "Just an attitude people have—two people work close together, they've *got* to be doing something wrong. Just can't work that close together and survive without being—doing *something*. It *galls* me. . . . But boy, since they've accused us we're sure having a ball!"

Occasionally supervisors and the women working for them adopt a flirtatious style, sharing occasional hugs, suggestive jokes, or playful romanticism. Innocuous to them ("All talk and no action, that's what I keep telling him!"), the style lends itself to gossip, which moreover is in some cases fully warranted. Paternal as well as flirtatious supervisors have on occasion pursued sexual relationships with women working for them. There is nothing peculiar to authority to mediate the generally charged atmosphere in which men and women interact. Excellent supervisors have become lovers to the women they care about, though rarely.

While some good supervisory relationships have sexual or quasi-sexual overtones, others verge on the paternal.[5] Women are of two minds about paternalistic bosses, so determined to see them succeed that they may protect them unnecessarily, sheltering them from the risks other workers confront and learn from: "And they want to see women do good, they really do—the ones I've worked with. And there's lots of times that they don't want to put you in different situations where they know you can't do it. Sometimes they have, like, a protective attitude."

Particularly in fire control, crew bosses are renowned for this feeling of paternal responsibility for "their girls," leading them to keep them from the hottest spots or the hardest tasks. This concern exceeds the natural care taken by good supervisors for their most inexperienced workers, many of whom are women. To some it seems a natural extention of their boss's evident concern and affection for them and is very gratifying—in addition to recognizing and accommodating what is often their very real lack of skill or developed strength. To others, excessive concern is patronizing, unwarranted, and unbearable. When the boss insists on women only taking a rest break while all others struggle on with heat and exhaustion, he singles her out on the basis of sex alone.

Good relationships with supervisors, then, are not uncomplicated.[6] Sometimes even the best of these sponsoring men are suspected of selfish (or at least unclear) motivation. Is she "his little protégé," designed to make him, not her, look good? Why exactly does he ask her to join the project team? He is encouraging, "*but* it was management that pushed all of this, so I don't know," though they wonder. And some are sensitive to unfair advantage: "You know, I'm going to move up fast, and I'm going to get a lot of favors handed my way, just because I make my ranger and other people look good. It's not *me*. It's some program that people . . . pushed, and they had to buy, you know what I mean?"

Some field workers feel themselves promoted, sponsored, and cultivated far beyond their own expectations or even desire. This is particularly true of professional women. Two foresters, both of whom see their future as less than settled and their options much broader than the Forest Service, explain:

> I guess the forest supervisor has identified me as someone who is going to be a district ranger. . . . See, I somehow have gotten into the good old boy system!

> Sometimes you almost get the feeling of getting pushed too fast. . . . They keep saying I'm going to be the first woman ranger. The guys over there at work even say it. I say, "Cut it out! I don't know about that!"

Others too feel the burden of supervisors' hopes and expectations and are anxious about finding a way to satisfy their own inclination and find the kind of career and level of commitment they prefer without at the same time hurting, showing up, or angering a boss who has gone out of his way to help and to encourage. Here too women complain of the sense of depersonalization which is the constant companion of the "token woman."

The differences are very clear between supervisors willing and able to deal fairly with women field workers and those to whom women present an unwanted burden, an intrusive and distracting presence. Bosses gain reputations as "empathetic" or "pushing women," or as the "nonpromoting, non-good-rating, don't-ask-him-to-do-anything-for-you" type. Some stand accused of trying to extort favors by withholding promised promotions, or of being rude and devious, or of blackballing "uppity" women. Some automatically rate women low on physical ability on the basis of principle rather than observation and must be directly confronted and persuaded to remove from the files such biased and damaging evaluations. Others disproportionately emphasize women's personality and attitude (e.g., "be less assertive") rather than technical skills and job performance.

Ideological opposition to women in the woods does not always imply bias as supervisors any more than verbal support guarantees fair treatment. Many men, including supervisors, are widely known as part of the "old guard" who on principle find women out of place in the woods. Yet such men gain respect for trying to deal with deep convictions of propriety and tradition: "His philosophy really was that a woman should stay home, but he said, 'Times are changing, and we've got to change with the times.' In fact, he tried setting up an all-woman crew. He's always gung-ho for that."

One man in particular stands out in this temporary field worker's mind when she thinks about the supervisors she has had the best luck with:

> He is so funny. He can sound real macho, and also the hard-core Forest Service man. But he is the *most* even, equitable supervisor that you have ever seen. . . . If he's standing around and somebody has to carry a pump up a hill, he'll turn around and say, "One of you take it up the hill." He doesn't care whether I do it or not. And a lot of people would say, "You, fellow, *you* carry that big pump up the hill for the little lady." He's also into letting people try—training, learning.

On another district, a different supervisor ignored a woman's report that she had painfully strained her back as a result of packing the pump once before to the bottom of a steep unit. (The pump is a portable water supply used in fire control. With water, hose, and other gear weighing up to ninety pounds, it is backpacked in and out of units being burned.) He insisted instead that she pack down a replacement pump and pack up the now malfunctioning pump which she had strained to carry down the day before. She lay in great pain, immobile, when at last she reached the landing and, after considerable struggle, won compensation for her permanent back injury and reinstatement in a different job. Her boss blamed her for "trying to be a man" and thus injuring herself deliberately. Generally two people together carry the pump; in this case there was only one person to do the job. The atmosphere in her district meant that her refusal to carry the weight the second and third times (after reporting an initial strain) might have cost her job.

The difference between supportive and resentful supervisors is critical, extending far beyond favors or small rebuffs to life-threatening situations. In a long hot summer of tension and mistrust, it was a crew boss and not a co-worker who threw one young woman to the ground and repeatedly booted her while the men of the crew gathered around to watch.

Job Training

With training, a woman can move up and away, and without it even the best intentions of the most sincere boss are meaningless. Permanent Forest Service employees are guaranteed forty hours of formal developmental training yearly beyond the amount necessary to do their job, for example, fire school or first aid classes. Some far exceed this amount of formal training, because of variation in available slots at the most popular training sessions. These classes are both contracted for and provided by Forest Service personnel, and range from the general (foremanship or management classes) to the specific (log scaling or contract writing).

Workers meet annually with their supervisors to draw up a mutually satisfactory yearly training plan (and here an informed and encouraging boss can be very helpful), but the best-laid plans sometimes go awry. Many have stories to tell of fighting fire on their first day of work or of being thrown cold into various situations. One woman can laugh now about her first day as a tree-planting inspector: "What happened was all the inspectors quit on them, and I was a new employee and the only one left, and they said, 'Here's a truck, here's a license, here's a tree, here's a map—go find this unit and have them plant it.'"

Women are often assumed to be transitory workers uninterested in long-term career development and thus inappropriate workers to train. They may also be seen as more difficult to train, lacking lifelong familiarity with the tools, language, and skills of the trade that many men bring to their work. Male supervisors have reportedly withheld training opportunities from animosity or disinclination to see women's careers prosper in their own immediate turf. More compliant women can be rewarded with the training denied obstreperous women.[7]

New workers do not always understand what it is they need to know; this is true both for formal and for on-the-job informal training. Informal learning may include instruction in outdoor survival, introduction to key actors and intrigues of the district, and insight into the kind of life the job involves—all as valuable as the lectures on equipment maintenance. Still, in many jobs, formal training is vital and there is no substitute for it. In this area career counseling (irregularly available, especially for temporary workers) can be of great value to women, making them knowledgeable about the required tests and classes which trip up others with less foresight.

Job progress depends as much on experience and informal learning as on formal training and certification, and they are all interrelated. Repeatedly, women stress that assertiveness—and initiative, organizational sophistication, and determination—are essential. For instance, resisting a natural inclination to accept special treatment and easier arrangements can later open new doors:

> If some supervisor—if you allow some supervisor to not give you the fair load, like heavy loads, lifting a lot of big equipment, things somebody on a fire crew is expected to do, then your chances of being channeled into

training that will help you in the future is a lot less. . . . And you've got to demand your right to be trained, in a way which brings you that training, because if you're not trained *here,* they're not going to train you *there.*

In precisely such an area a woman's boss can help and hurt. One summer a woman working for a man with traditional ideas about female capabilities did not once run the chain saw. A new boss arrived, and the next season was very different: "He expected me to know how to run a chain saw, and so he *made* me get out there and run it. And I came to enjoy running it, and have gotten more confident with it."

Sometimes sheer persistence pays off. Persistence indeed was demanded of the woman who, despite excellent scores, was tested and retested three times at the request of offices progressively farther up the line before her certification in a skill long considered exclusively male was accepted and she could begin work at last. Another determined woman eventually was sent to chain saw school:

> I always watched. I was really interested, because I wanted to learn as much as I could. So I always talked and asked everybody questions at lunch—how this, and how did they decide that. And when [he] was out cleaning the chain saw and stuff, I would sit there and watch him, ask him how he does it and how does he know, and he'd sit there and explain it all to me and everything.

Women agree on the importance of speaking out, asking questions, and showing interest, but those who know must be willing to share what they know. Very often men are reluctant to pass on information or share ideas; instead they protect their insider's knowledge and skill, regarding it as the power resource it is. Complaints are common about men who clam up when women are around, and who cannot or will not take the time to demonstrate rather than take over, or to explain the process of reasoning behind a decision. A boss who constantly wonders "what else can I show you? what do you need to know?" stands apart from one who prefers silence or is still learning how to teach. "When you're learning something, you have to know something about it in order to ask a question. And if I'd say, 'I've done it this way,' he'd say 'OK.' But what I was looking for was 'Well, have you tried this?' Or, 'You could have done this'—something more helpful. And that took a long time, to really be able to sit down and talk."

When an inexperienced worker unfamiliar with the work process, the tools, the surroundings, perhaps even the language in use asks for help, the response that follows is critical. One new field worker recalls her frustration: "I felt very uncomfortable because I hadn't ever been in the woods, and there was an awful lot I knew I didn't know. And I needed to depend on those guys to teach me, and they're coming across as if they expect me to know everything, and I don't. And I can't get it across to them—'I *don't* know what this is, I *don't* know what to do. Help me!'"

Male silence can stem from ignorance. Men may be incapable of answering a woman's questions and may be unable to acknowledge it for fear of exposing their own ignorance, to her and to the boss. Other times they are simply unaware of the gap of knowledge and ability: "And the man doesn't mean to not teach it to her, but it was never really taught to him. It was just something he kind of learned because he was around it. . . . I feel like that happens a lot, where the men don't *mean* to keep the information from us. They just don't necessarily know how to convey or know that it even needs to be."

One young technician's story sums up many of these themes. Her first woods job put her on a tanker crew with two men, to whom she was pleasant company and not much more: "They *really* did not want to teach me. I mean, there were people who actually said no to me—you know, 'I'm not going to show you, find out from somebody else.'" Throughout the season these two assumed responsibility for most of the work. She learned little—and nothing at all about the operation of the water pumper truck: "Always, as soon as you got to a fire, they just *took over*— 'Grab the hose and run!' And so I *never* got the experience."

When her prior experience placed her the next season on a different tanker crew, it was assumed that she was a competent operator of the pumper, an assumption she found it easier to let pass than to correct. She was humiliated later in the summer when her skill was tested in a crunch, and her supervisor had to help, thus advertising her surprising ignorance. She talks about the experience, which has led her both to try to speak up and to decline a job offer which would place her in a supervisory position:

> And there are *so* many times when I feel intimidated and don't ask questions. And it gets worse too, because I keep going up in rating, and lots of times I don't find out these things, and I don't think that I really assume the responsibility that I should. It's like, I keep putting it off, because I really don't want to let them know that I don't know that much! And then it gets worse and worse. . . . And I don't think I have any business being in a position like that [as crew boss], you know, until I find out what I'm doing. And at the same time, I find it . . . , I find myself being real passive in a lot of situations, and it really makes me angry, because I don't learn.

This honesty and sense of responsibility help explain why many supervisors say they prefer women to men on their crews. They find them trustworthy and conscientious, quicker to ask questions and slower to take offense at suggestions. Often they are fast learners, less hostile than men to supervision, and are highly motivated workers. A supervisor's positive experience with some women field workers sets the stage for a positive approach to other women, in a mutually reinforcing positive cycle as influential as is the reverse.

While male resistance to training women co-workers has many roots, we can identify some of the social conditions making this kind of conflict more and less likely. For instance, structural conflict inherent in the work process and job structures encourages sexual conflict, as when old-time field technicians must train well-educated professionals with little woods sense or familiarity with local terrain. This endemic structural conflict intensifies when sexual status and professional status are at odds. One well-known fiasco involved a long-term male technician charged with providing foresters with the on-the-job training they need. This is often a tense relationship (e.g., "as a technician versus a professional, I'd like to tell him where to put it"), with professional mobility and technical immobility at its root. Professional foresters move up quickly, from a GS-5 to a GS-9 in as little as two years. This time the professional was a woman, one of the first female foresters ever, and her boss could not or would not teach her his trade. As a male observer notes: "He let her look as bad as he made her be." She was happy to transfer away shortly and most of those in the unit were happy to see her go.

Women fare better in the company of a "green" crew, benefiting by the presence of similarly ignorant men. The mobility of the work force also facilitates the instruction of new workers, male or female. Skills must be passed on successfully, although in entry-level jobs the necessary training may be perfunctory: "Everybody just got out of the crummy, and I go, 'what do you do?' and he goes, 'pick up sticks.' So I started picking up sticks!" Safety also demands minimal training of all workers (especially in fire crews), and self-interest if nothing else encourages old-timers to teach newcomers more than what they learn at fire school about the art of fire fighting: "Nobody wants a cull next to them out there."

Opposition to training women comes from co-workers and supervisors, from old-timers and young men even newer than women to the job, and from the "mellow" and the ex-Marine alike. It springs from an inability to accept women workers as peers and is an effective mechanism in the protection of male competence and control. These men create a legacy of bitterness among the women woods workers they meet.

Women Supervising Men

When women in turn supervise and train, the tensions are exacerbated. More striking than the occasional successes are the wrenching and disheartening failures which so quickly enter organizational lore and form the context in which each new woman supervisor works. Most experiences fall somewhere between these two extremes, and as women supervisors become more common, this more neutral middle ground is likely to prevail.

Women are rarely appointed crew bosses, though many do have the length and breadth of experience of male crew bosses. When a woman does become an effective crew boss, her authority may not be recognized formally. The routine duties but not the nominal title were gladly conferred on one woman by the man ostensibly in charge, who preferred to work instead with a nearby friend, but it was left to her to translate this supervisory experience to paper. Other women too have had to fight for the formal training and certification they need to make their on-the-ground experience count in their files too.

The organizational oral history records women supervisors generally as disasters. Men go over their heads to appeal to male authority and deliberately ignore or circumvent directions. Women bosses are cursed and yelled at and an occasional fist is shaken in their faces. Men complain of a woman's style of supervision, her technical judgment, and her qualifications as crew boss. All these problems arise most particularly when she is a forceful, visible supervisor. So many women assume background roles, adopt "easygoing" styles, encourage group decisions (e.g., flipping coins), and avoid confrontation. The following description is typical: "There's not a lot you could do. I didn't have any power and I didn't want to throw any power around. I didn't want to make a big power play out of it. . . . Nobody was really wanting to work real hard, so everybody just kind of took it easy. We got the work done but just didn't do it gung-ho."

Men encourage women to be "straw bosses."[8] They may also try to make the female boss something else entirely. She may be cast as a mother figure to whom they appeal for health care hints and sympathy. Or perhaps she is treated as a sexual object, "too cute to take seriously" as a boss, but there for them to routinely flirt with, try to date, and freely touch.

The support of those who gave them authority originally is essential to women supervisors. Each one must know her decisions will be backed up and her authority legitimated. But sometimes male supervisors find themselves more in sympathy with the men who are unable to accept the female boss. One woman active in civil rights programs was outraged by this:

> The men came in and said, "We won't work with a woman." And they [management] came to me and said, "Well, what will we do?" And I said, "Damn it, you know the system as well as I do. They don't have the option to say they won't work with a woman! You document it. *You* make out her performance rating, not her crew—black, white, or Godzilla in drag. They don't get to make the decision of who they work for. They work for *us*. And we assign the crew bosses and we assign the work." And it's amazing to me that a GS-11 supervisor *didn't know* that they didn't have the option. Now, if it was a black man . . . !

To some men a woman is by definition an illegitimate boss. More often the potential for sexual conflict is aggravated by structural conflicts. For example, most field crews are beset with personality conflicts and interpersonal struggles of various kinds (some notoriously so), and this is certainly the case when the boss is a woman. Few minority men work in field positions, but on occasion the issue has been a black man's resentment of supervision by "a white wench." An early field-going woman remembered her worst opposition:

> The only trouble I had was with guys fresh home from Nam. Well, I knew the rest of them, most of them were local people, and the ones that weren't showed up and I was there so—what the hell. But I was just as fair—you know, I never asked anything more of them. If I wouldn't do it myself, I wouldn't ask anybody else to do it. At first there was a lot of . . . standoffishness. And a lot of—they'd go and ask somebody else if they really had to do what I said. . . . And the guys fresh home from Nam said they'd been taking orders all their goddamned life, and by God, they weren't about to do it from no *woman*.

The endemic conflicts rooted in organizational status (e.g., the technician vs. the professional) contribute to the shouting matches and painful silences which so often mar these early experiences with female authority. Sometimes the problem is rooted in women's inexperience in the field. Their formal education and grade may give them priority over male co-workers when supervisory assignments are made though they may be fairly new to the area or job. Though otherwise the most qualified person for the job, the woman may have less experience in the woods generally. She may simply be a newcomer and outsider, fighting many battles at once when she prematurely becomes the boss of a crew of strangers. One woman recounts her disastrous experience when she was suddenly appointed foreman of a crew including a man thrice passed over by his superior for just that privilege.

A woman boss can be harder on the women working for her, recognizing the interdependence of all female newcomers: "I worked too hard to get my job to let some of them twitches screw it up." Crews with many women are sometimes reported to be more attuned to male authority once or twice removed than to their immediate female boss, in precisely the same way that some men evade direct female authority.

Promotion for failure is a strategy successfully used against men and women alike, but the visibility of female failure makes it more destructive for women. One woman was just twenty-one, looked younger, and was not yet adjusted to the work demands. She had no supervisory training, nor was she sure she even wanted it: "It's just that it's really the only way in the government to go up in the world." She summed up her experience.

> I've never really had to sit out there and produce physical labor under bad weather, steep terrain, that kind of thing. It wasn't easy . . . and I was working with men who could handle it. . . . They would just sit and pick on me, just kind of make a fool of me, pick on me, to the point that I would just sit out there and cry on occasion. . . . And here I am out there making a lot of mistakes. And they *knew* it. I mean, shoot, it was hard to hide what was going on!

Some women feel power and control over others is not their "style" nor particularly their preference and struggle each day with their own ambivalence: "And I *do* know what's going on out there, whether or not I like to admit it. I think I'm capable of it, if I just would assume more responsibility. But it . . . it scares me, a lot of times. . . . But at the same time, I found that the men that I was supervising lots of times were real supportive."

Spectacular failures are few, but very influential. In one instance work ground to a halt because of repeated confrontations between the largely male crew, the female supervisor, and the women assistants she appointed. Several male workers complained bitterly about the women and regularly refused direction. Despite her accommodating attitude, the assistant crew boss felt the pain of sheer defiance:

> Yeah, but I didn't really care, because, like I say, I didn't really want to be. I didn't ask to be crew boss, I just did it because they didn't have anybody else to do it that they wanted to appoint. And I *could* have said, "OK, buddy, get

in the truck, we're going back to the station, this is it for you." I could have done that, but it just wasn't that important to me. I know I'm not a good boss. I'm not the boss-type person. To me, it didn't make any difference whether we started at this end of the unit or at that end of the unit. I mean, if they wanted to do that, fine. But they just . . . seemed like sometimes they'd just want to do different from what I said. . . . Sometimes I would just say, "*OK*, let's *do* that side first." There'd be times when I'd feel like they were really just trying to make trouble. And I didn't like it. But other times I just didn't care.

The summer dragged on unpleasantly. Dissension spread throughout the group amid charges of favoritism and incompetence, and turnover was high. The boss spent most of her time hiring and training new workers, fielding complaints, and parrying insults. Supportive observers attempted to help by speaking publicly of supervisory authority to report insubordination, but several women felt such actions only exaggerated the "them and us" atmosphere which was so destructive. No men were fired, although today the supervisor faults herself for being reluctant to fire for insubordination.

In contrast, her experience during the next season was extremely positive. Again she was crew boss but also a working member of the crew, the only woman, and effectively a "straw boss" on a crew of self-directing, somewhat older, more experienced men. They organized their work informally, working independently and cooperatively, and she was no longer responsible for hiring and firing. It was easy for all to forget that she was nominally in charge. The downplay of direct authority helps women manage male hostility and resentment. It may be that the low-key style of supervision so often described by women is also their only real option; for them, nothing else works.

The problems women supervisors face demand their very best, and their ambivalence reflects an uneasy understanding of the difficulties ahead. But for every woman defeated, and there have been notable cases, others will take her place. One thoughtful woman announced her future career plans unabashedly: "to have men working for *me!*" Across the table her elderly mother-in-law grinned and raised her hands in silent cheers. This part of the story is really just beginning.

Contract Inspection

What about female contract inspectors, those women who follow the contract crews planting trees or building roads, to ensure that organizational standards are met? Overall, their experience is more positive. A contract inspector's power base is fundamentally strong: she represents the authority of the employing organization; her evaluation of the work determines (within contract guidelines) the money contractors make; it is in her power to stop work altogether if necessary; and her bird's-eye view as the front-line supervisor influences the reputation and future employment prospects of the contract crew. Her authority is tangible, as she observes contract workers and notes wage-determining irregularities in their work. Although inspectors must be able to do the job they supervise, in this role they are observers; the female contract inspector is not in direct control over others but manages the work in conjunction with the male contractor. She is still at some remove from men with organizational power who are sensitive to male prerogative and are able to defend it.

The relationship between contract crews and Forest Service inspectors is often contentious, with conflicts of interest overlaying ideological differences—the logger versus the environmentalist, for example, or small business versus government bureaucracy. Inspectors can assume that initially their ability and attitude will be thoroughly tested, and women inspectors are considered an easy mark.

Some women do report a transitional testing period, including flirting by "old geezers." They may rely initially on the established reputation of their predecessors to ease the way. Trained and introduced by him, they enter under his auspices: "Oh, if I thought I had to go in there cold!" one young inspector exclaimed.

The female inspector may, like the woman quoted below, use the contractors as her primary learning tool:

> Those guys have been in the business for twenty-five years, most of them, and there's *no* point in trying to convince them that you know more than they do! So you sit back and listen. And I found that the majority of them are just aching to tell somebody, and teach you all they know about it. So I picked their brains! And I can just learn *tons* from him, if I just let him. But if I would pretend that I knew more than what I knew, I'd be in trouble.

She may also use the contractor's prejudices, relying at least temporarily on his uncertainty about her response to conflict:

> But some of them, with the male inspectors, of course they'll get obnoxious and mad and upset. You know, sometimes there can be some conflict there. And they'll be pretty verbal and vocal and tell them where to go, and where to stuff it. . . . And I haven't encountered that either yet, but—see, they still treat us women with kind of kid gloves out there, because they're not quite

sure how we're going to react. And I'd just as soon keep it that way! They don't know whether I'll break down and cry, or what!

Though she may be half the contractor's age and half his height, a woman inspector relies on all of these factors—and especially on her own competence and confidence—to maintain the organizational standards. She also cultivates the businesslike demeanor adopted by the best male inspectors, to defuse the more personal relationship some contract workers or subcontractors attempt. This professionalism can take the sting out of deliberate stunts intended to shock and distract, including public love making and defecating, intense staring, or flirtatious chatter.

Sometimes managers and professionals doubt women's ability to maintain an appropriate professional distance. Some even fear for women's safety, insisting that "it gets rough out there" when contractors and inspectors argue. Men worry particularly when women inspectors work with Mexican crews or near loggers, though women inspectors report no unusual problems. On the other hand, some men hint that attractive women inspectors may be the best choice for the job: "The contractors will do anything she asks! They just like to see her come around."

Many of the contract workers in the woods bring very traditional attitudes to work, and women find in them some of the most deep-rooted and intractable opposition. Still, as contract work grows in importance in the organization and women increasingly join the ranks of those inspecting others' work, a solid base for the future grows—for time and again the story ends well. One old seaman now building roads for the Forest Service and dealing with a woman inspector for the first time had this to say after he knew her a while: "'You know, I've never worked for a woman out here in the field,' he says. 'It's coffee-break time, but I don't drink coffee. I usually have a chew,' he says, 'so I guess I'm going to have to offer you a chew.' And I thanked him, because I felt that everything was all right. I declined but thanked him for it!"

The routine disparagement of the Forest Service by the contract workers they employ is not challenged but reinforced when the inspectors are women too. Work done by women is taken as less masculine in the continuing invidious comparison of prowess between the independent logger and the "forest technician" of the Forest Service. Increasing numbers of women contract inspectors confirm the low status of government workers relative to those who do the work the government only monitors.[9] As sexual and organizational status converge, men may begin to avoid work as contract inspectors. As yet, the issues raised by female authority in field work have not been fully confronted for lack of experience.

Summary

In this chapter some of the parameters of women field workers' experiences have been defined—how they typically enter the organization and are distributed throughout it, how sexual stereotyping is maintained, how they handle authority and how their bosses handle them.

Getting the outdoor job in the first place proves the first of a series of challenges to full-fledged participation in woods work. Sometimes women enter field work circuitously; the permanent job especially is elusive for women. Once employed they find themselves limited to work and responsibility deemed compatible with femininity, although the boundaries are variously defined and enforced. Spontaneous stereotyping emerges in the casual division of labor within crews or between partners. The mobility of new women field workers is limited by these patterns and by their own intentions and ambitions.

The men who supervise women are instrumental in providing the kind of training women need to work well and to progress. They also set the tone by which a woman is received by others, including male workers whose help is essential in informal training. Organizational sponsorship of women by key supervisors is not uncommon nor without problems. Control over the work of others largely remains in the hands of men. Women's experience with supervision over colleagues is limited, and female authority is more easily accepted at some distance, as in contract inspection.

4

Shoulder to Shoulder:
Models of Accommodation

In the beginning, the daily work life of women and men in the field revolves around carving out satisfactory ways of working together. Men wonder who exactly stands alongside—looking for all the world like any other worker but clearly and ineffably different. Women wonder what is expected of them and how they will meet the challenges ahead. Together, in the best case, they forge ways of working together in the woods, an important step in the interminably long and complex process of occupational desegregation.

Special meaning always attaches to the small gestures, the smiles and snickers and the helping hand, and in the early stages of women's entry into field work much of it reflects the familiar dynamic of testing and proving, probing the newest worker for strengths and weaknesses, aptitude and attitude. What is her approach to the job, to authority, to other workers? Will she prove to be a slacker or a rate buster? Does she carry herself self-consciously or easily, smile freely or only rarely open up? She is tested in light of her female predecessor, if there was one. Will she be as good a worker or as lax? Is she as large, as cute, or as friendly? Will she prove more like Fran the Feminist or Fanny the Flirt? In groups so lopsidedly masculine, the female newcomer's ability and attitude are evaluated generically and come to represent the limitations and capabilities of the gender. Rarely does she have the privilege of self-definition and peculiarity in a situation where the salience of gender makes her every move or gesture representative, at least initially.[1]

Many women report being informed by well-intentioned supervisors that they owed their job to their sex, a feeling they very much resent. They are "tokens" employed to fulfill some remote management objective or pacify some fleeting liberal urge and are so informed. Some are told, though rarely is it necessary, that they will be carefully watched or that the future of women in the district, job, or crew depends on their performance. Like solo women on all-male crews, women "firsts," true path breakers on all-male turf, find the burdens of visibility painfully direct. Other women also face the surveillance and monitoring and judicious testing and probing. By and large they are very much aware of it, whether they are proclaimed districtwide as "guinea pigs" or are more covertly watched.

One hears that "culls"—rejects from prime timber that are tossed aside as waste—are found in both sexes, and it is a principal task in any work group to evaluate the newcomer. This process varies in intensity and importance. For example, in "laid-back" crews a newcomer's attitude toward drugs is important to establish, and during fire season, physical strength, stamina, and spirit will be tested immediately. For women in traditionally male and physically demanding jobs, there is always a special quality to this commonplace aspect of work life and small group behavior. The fundamental fact of a woman's minority status in sex-skewed groups and thus her extreme visibility as a generic representative of the sex lend a certain intensity and symbolism to the testing of new women field workers.

Women new to the job are checked out in numerous ways, beginning with at least a cursory physical evaluation and rating by male co-workers who proclaim as "natural" their interest in appearance, demeanor, and apparent sexual availability. On an all-male work crew or work site her arrival may be something of an event. One woman described her relationships with heavy equipment operators when she and her male partner arrive in the area:

> Well, you always get the feeling that when you come on the scene, you "come on the scene." Like, "There's a woman out there!" Because there are none, there are absolutely none. The only time that any of these guys see any is when they go home. . . . So when I get out there everybody shuts down. They might normally do that when anybody goes out, but to me it's like—"Who's *in* there?!" And a lot of them say, "Well, aren't you going to introduce me to your helper?" and all this other stuff.

Occasionally the "Queen Bee" syndrome sets in when solo women on male crews come to enjoy their special status. Though more often another woman newcomer is greeted warmly, as someone to share lunch with or simply to "bitch about the men with," at least one experienced hand ruefully admitted her initial jealousy—"Hey, this is *my* territory!" Relations with other women are complicated, primarily by lack of per-

sonal contact but also by their shared minority status. About equal numbers explicitly reject the unfair burden they feel of "the weight of
womankind" and resent the constant comparison with the other lone
woman down the road, as, alternatively, feel a real sense of history and
responsibility to other women:

> Definitely, definitely I feel a woman has to do a much better job to even be
> acknowledged, much less to get anything extra. And I feel like—yeah, I feel
> like every single day the women are struggling. They're not just there doing
> a job. They're there setting the standards for what it's going to be like for
> other women in the Forest Service. It's real important how we conduct
> ourselves in everything, because people generalize. They'll say, "OK, we had
> a woman do that once, and she couldn't do it."

Whether or not they resent their link with other women, most tire of
the attention and the pressures of visibility. Who can say how many
women field workers have left their jobs precisely because of this burden? For some the pressure is almost too much, and promotion or
transfer is no relief:

> *All* the time, all the time . . . I've never been so defensive in my life as when
> I started with the Forest Service. And my defenses have risen so much. It's
> like I always had to prove myself. I don't think I'm proving myself any
> longer. I think I'm going to have to maybe, if I get this [GS-] 7. . . . You've
> always got to *prove* yourself to these people, like you can do it, you know.
> And if you've had a really bad day, with all the pressures from the job and
> everything—God, don't let them see it! And there's been times I've broken
> down.

These women's lives are endlessly complicated by the imputation of
generality to their every movement and the close inspection it entails.
They complain of bosses who "hover" near them and only them, and of
co-workers who sit on landings "and watch you hike out of a unit just to
see how fast you can go—you just feel it, you know it." Work may be
checked and rechecked if done by a woman, and eyebrows may be raised
if her work keeps her indoors a day or two and she appears out of field
garb. They feel the lack of freedom to err and the pressure of always
being on display:

> It's an extreme load, it really is. Because I feel I've got to be up all the time.
> If I make a mistake, everybody's really going to pounce on it. Where a guy,
> he can have his down days, he can make mistakes. . . . That's just the way it
> is. Basically, the first few years, more or less any time you're a woman that

you sit down and start taking things a little bit easier, they say, "Yeah, look at these women, sitting down. They just can't do the job." And it really is a feeling that's there—women are still being watched.

These first days and weeks can be nervewracking, and many women nurse physical symptoms of stress and anxiety to complement aching muscles unused to exercise. They return home bone weary from matching strides all day with long-legged men who take hills "like a little deer" and make them feel like "rug rats" by comparison. There often comes a moment of truth, when this is seen as the test it is and hence is suddenly intelligible. One woman tells the story of her first fire, when her long-haired male partner blithely led her to believe it was her job to carry all the hose down into the unit—and she believed him. Only later was she set straight by an older man who clarified the limits of her responsibility. More than one woman has a similar story to tell: "They tried to put me through the paces. They told me afterwards, about a year later. And I thought this was the way they worked all the time! At times I was glad it was raining because I was just about ready to cry. . . . I found that after a about a week and a half they slowed down considerably. And at first I thought, 'Boy, I'm getting used to it,' and then I found out *they* were slowing down!"

At the same time, no test can also be a test of sorts, when women face lower expectations and standards. Amazement is expressed at female competence—bettering a man's pace through the brush, successfully parrying a quarrelsome camper, scoring well on technical examinations— just as the familiar backhanded compliment "pretty good for a woman" is still heard. Women field workers must meet these and other problems head-on, gracefully, and during an initial period of uncertainty and stress. This period of overt testing is transitory, though it is a threshold some women never move completely beyond.

Both women and men, low- and high-status workers, tend to concur on one point: women try harder. They are highly motivated to perform, and when they fail it is not for lack of heart. They must prove themselves graciously, conveying both their ability and the appropriate attitude preferred by their co-workers;

> I try extra hard. I always do more than them—sort of makes the guys feel funny at first! Because I try so hard. . . . But the only reason I do is to make sure I *can* do my part. And I think they understand that that's the only reason I work so hard, is just so I won't be a burden to them. . . . [At the beginning of each new season] it's usually an inspiration to them—they want to do better! And I've had a few foremen say that's good, they like to see

that. Because they know the guys can do it, and they said that it's good that
they at least have a little inspiration to do it, because at first motivation isn't
too good, you know . . . no one wants to start into all that stuff again.

Women report keeping back tears and denying blisters or aching
muscles, always careful to hide fear or self-doubt or discouragement.
Walking with men may force a faster pace than comes naturally, but
when all pause at the top of the ridge a woman will disguise her heavy
breathing; should she be the first one up, she will carefully explain her
bicycle-riding regimen of recent months. Later they can laugh at mem-
ory-making scenes from this early period. One permanent woman recalls
the grueling all-day hike she took with a number of professional men, for
whom it was "their one big time to show off how speedily they can go
through the forest." Despite her determined efforts she was the last one
in and the last one out, precisely the situation women try so hard to
avoid: "Well, I knew that would happen. Of course, they all go—zoom!—
through the forest. They've all got longer legs than I do. They can get up
on the trees by going hop-skip. I have to hoist myself up on top, swing my
legs over, and come back down the tree. I'm slower." Eventually she took
a different course, agreeing to meet the group later on. The gruesome
day ended when she finally arrived to find them already in the van and
waiting for her. Before their very eyes, "I went to make a flying leap
down the embankment and fell in a heap!"

Occasionally the traditional "battle of the sexes" is joined, when determined women work near men sensitive to the challenge of female competence. "Woods jocks" in particular take their work very seriously. One
woman remembers watching her new male partner gulp down candy
bars for extra energy, to guarantee (she felt sure) that he would be the
one to set the pace. The sheer presence of women seems to spur certain
men to extra effort—an unintended consequence of female integration
which amuses women and delights supervisors. Overtly sex-based competition is sometimes tolerated or even encouraged. Some couples take
this challenge so to heart that work is impossible; for example, when
working the survey chain they pull so hard on their respectively female
and male ends that only a "tug of war" results. More commonly the
impetus to competition is discouraged. Men and women react differently
to the competition and its results, as one woman notes: "Oh, for myself, I
don't mind being beaten by a man, because it's been confronted—I
mean, it happens to me all the time! I mean, you can't mind it or you
would be beating your head against the wall. But the men—hey! it really
bothers them."

Some managers, bosses, and co-workers are sensitive to the pressures
on women constantly "behind the eight ball," as one ranger put it, even as

they acknowledge their own inclination to watch women more closely. Men who monitor women's performance very often see what they mean to see. A unit manager skeptical of women's physical ability to keep up reports that men often "carry" a woman, although to his surprise they do so cheerfully. Another manager dedicated to seeing field women succeed notes the way a female forester was nearly "walked into the ground" on her first day, but he is confident of the transitory nature of this extreme testing and of her ability to measure up. Some men familiar with training sessions for supervisors report explicit admonishments to watch the performance of women on the crew carefully.

With some important exceptions, most men interviewed displayed a remarkable naivete about the consequences of minority status. To them the testing period is universal and benign, though some concede women may be watched a bit more carefully at first. The positions of the sexes seem essentially interchangeable. One young man, for instance, equates his freedom as a juggler to wander around project fire camps of hundreds of fire fighters with women's essentially equal freedom of mobility; after all, no one hassled him for being somewhat out of the ordinary. Older supervisors in particular are more sensitive to the special burdens of gender and to the history of male opposition and resistance to women in field work.

The Physical Test: The Case of Women Fire Fighters

Of all the unanswered questions surrounding the introduction of new women field workers, one of the most pressing concerns physical ability and a woman's attitude toward accepting help. This is true whether she takes a job walking survey lines, cruising timber, doing tree inventories, or inspecting trails. In one instance the issue may be the speed with which she can walk through the woods, in another the agility with which she handles cumbersome and heavy equipment. In each case expectations are relative to the job and the prevailing standards of the particular crew, district, or supervisor of the moment. Because of the rigors of fire fighting and because so many female newcomers work as temporaries in the fire organization, the questions are posed most keenly and persistently for women fire fighters. Regardless of job assignment, most field workers will be in fire situations sometime during their careers. Because the case against women field workers is often made in this context, the physical test of women fire fighters touches all women in the organization.

The prevention and control of forest fires is close to a shared creed, and most want to take part in it. For some it is thrilling work; to others it simply offers contrast to the daily grind, a kind of outing and a lucrative change of pace. Some men find it incredible good luck ("I can get dirty and get paid for it!") while others take a more philosophical view: "I used to enjoy fires . . . [Seriously burned one season, he no longer fights fire.] in the sense that it had a *cause* to it. You were protecting nature! That's kind of a funky way to put it, but that's where it's at—to protect the environment . . . and to be a fire fighter. To say, you know, 'I was a fire fighter.'"

Many share the exhilaration of hard, purposeful work fighting the essential uncertainty of natural forces. There is a "low margin for error," and lives are risked and sometimes lost before the fire is contained. The spirit is satisfying and binds together groups of very different people, as this young woman discovered during her first project fire:

> It was something, because I've heard of fires being a real drag, but this was great. I mean really, we just had fun. We had a good group. You get to really talking to people, out there looking at the stars, and you get into these deep conversations. You really look out for each other. And you spend every waking hour with that crew—it can drive you nuts! Some of the people you get to wishing you could strangle, but . . . it was a good experience for me.

Only workers meeting minimal physical standards can fight fire. To protect the weak, and those whose responsibility they become, all workers must take a standardized test of physical capacity and endurance under stress. The "step test" (built around timed performance up and down steps) ranks recovery rate following short-term exertion. Those testing above a certain point may attend off-forest project fires; those scoring higher can be assigned fire line duty once they are there. Intended only as a guide to distinguish the fit from the less fit, the test is roundly criticized as inaccurate and fundamentally irrelevant to the demands of a fire situation. Women's generally adequate performance seems simply to support the critics' case, while to others it publicly indicates the competitive physical ability of women. The test will be outdated before the arguments. Pressure continues to mount for a more discretionary test of strength, agility, and endurance (involving an obstacle course, pull-ups, and other tests). The likely consequences for women are a subject of controversy and concern.

Some women who otherwise do demanding physical work draw the line at fire fighting. They are uncertain about their own physical limits and do not want them tested during a time of danger. Those with husbands and children sometimes find the demands on the family too much, while others simply resent having to "turn over an unlimited period of time" to attend project fires.

When forest fires cannot be contained by local labor, project fires are declared, and regional management teams organize militarylike encampments for the masses of hardy fire fighters who may be airlifted in from any corner of the country. Many at camp work in management, staff, or service positions. Building fire line is grueling work, with limitations imposed on duty shifts, conditions of rest and meals, consecutive hours of labor, and so forth. Women and men alike return to camp bone weary and unrecognizably filthy, eat a quick bite, and drop into their (disposable) paper sleeping bags for precious hours of sleep. With the others on their crew they work, eat, and sleep in a fog of smoke and exhaustion, uncertain about the state of the fire, how things go at home, their likely departure date, or even when their next chance to grab a shower may come.[2]

In the recent past, project fire camps were renowned for hard-working, hard-living, "line-building, fire-fighting, he-men," with drinking, fighting, and prostitution all part of the scene. Fire fighters seem to fancy themselves "ferocious, rough and tough and rugged." It can be a convivial atmosphere as friends separated by transfer meet during a break or travel time; sometimes there is a moment for campfire songs and the recounting of fires past and the big ones fought. "Camp followers" of the past knew a likely source of business when they saw it, giving a history to the persistent rumors about sex at fire camp.[3]

Like other inherently risky, physically demanding jobs performed under unpredictable and largely uncontrollable conditions, fire fighting is surrounded by a self-serving mythology. Fire suppression crews pride themselves on their elite status; in the Northwest only a limited number exist, and in the past they have been dominated by military men with a reputation for ruggedness. Those few workers fighting fire visibly and heroically from the air outshine the "ground stompers" with their more routine contribution.

As the major preoccupation of the organization, forest fire control has a central place ideologically and far exceeds in oral history and memory its actual frequency. Far more common (and more dangerous, some workers add) is the routine work of the field season, the clearing of the land following logging operations to prepare for burning refuse and eventual replanting—"doing the job necessary to make little trees grow again."

Contained burns lack the excitement and "camping trip" atmosphere of the project fire. Those whose job is "stacking sticks" all summer may actually move and pile heavy timbers, use power saws all day long, and carry flame-dripping torches spreading fire all around them, fighting extreme heat and sometimes exhaustion too. At other times their enemy is monotony and tedium as they sit for hours after fires are contained, alert for the tiniest recurring smoke or spark.

The job must be done, so when all conditions are right, slash burning begins, and it ends only when the fire is out. Every worker of any tenure has tales to tell of burns beginning in early dawn and ending late at night, with only a light lunch to hold them—a grueling day ending either with a celebratory beer with the others or a quick few hours of sleep before beginning yet another day of burning. Because they must be fit and strong and because apparently only their bodies are taxed, brush disposal crews earn reputations as "brush dummies" or "big dummies." In fact their work is longer, quite as difficult, and all the more dangerous for being routine, unlike those heroic gatherings at project fire camps to fight the big fire.

Though it is a powerful and entrenched department, fire control and fire fighters have their detractors. They "think they *are* the Forest Service" one worker grumbles, though their work is seasonal, perhaps even outdated if wildfires are allowed to burn again, and mainly demanding of brute force. One female critic vividly expresses feelings many share:

> They're a cross between a football team and a military regiment! Very male, very regimented. . . . "We eat babies for lunch. We go into town and rape women on weekends." You know—no shit! This is the way they are. And they promote people for their male aggressive abilities. But I've seen them on the fire line and they don't work that goddamned much harder than everybody else—they're just dumber! They *run* everywhere.

Technicians dominate in fire control, and those at the helm are often men whose credentials are years of field experience rather than years of college. In an outfit priding itself on professionalism, fire seems peculiarly provincial and traditional. One unit manager puts the common argument very bluntly when he hints at a class difference between fire and timber employees: "They are a lower—I don't like to use this word, but they are a lower caliber person in the fire game, for some reason. I don't know why. That's where your problems are [personnel problems, bad debts, minor crimes, alcohol, and drug abuse]. . . . They want to work six months and they want to play six months of the year. They're not interested in working year-round."

This stereotype of fire fighters, and it is important to remember it is a stereotype, also includes fierce opposition to women co-workers. The "crude and lewd" do not take kindly to fighting fire alongside women. Fire management officers refuse (or attempt to avoid) women on their front-line crews, depriving women of the experience and contacts they need. Rules are enforced to discourage women. The mandated all-cotton fire wardrobe, for example, makes some women uncomfortable because they cannot find all-cotton brassieres. As she prepared to step into the helicopter carrying fire fighters to a distant fire, one embarrassed woman had to give her bra to someone suddenly intent upon enforcing the rule.

Some critics can accept women at home where they can help with slash burning but draw the line at project fires. The sturdy worker with good rapport with her fellow slash burners rejected her boyfriend's jokes that she was really simply their "mascot" until the day even her best friends turned against her and discouraged her attendance at fire camp. Her persistence brought her a place at camp but notoriety as well, for she was ordered off the fire line the second day because of a "foot injury" she did not have. While a complaint and investigation won her the right to work on the fire line, she lost half her supporters in the process and shortly began to look for work elsewhere.

Many factors are at work in the well-known opposition to women fire fighters. Fire control has more experience dealing with women than many other departments; by contrast, for instance, managers voicing their support for women in the Forest Service have virtually no firsthand experience with women peers. The unit manager whose fire management officer insists that women simply cannot measure up wonders aloud if pride is really the issue. And perhaps men in fire, often lacking college educations themselves, feel uncomfortable working with women as educated as Forest Service women often are. Defense of a satisfying self-image locating masculinity in physical prowess may also be implicated. Both an administrator and a field-working woman make the same point:

It's the last macho department they have, you know! They start putting women in there, they lose all that—that's supposedly in there.

I think a lot of the problem is that they sit there and they tell themselves how tough they are, that they can do this work. And they look—and I'm obviously not a very strong, tough person, I'm also small—they look over and see a 110-pound person doing the work that they're doing. And you can't tell yourself that you're really strong, you're really great, if you see somebody like that.

In fire as elsewhere, ridicule from the other men of the forest can hurt; loggers sometimes taunt Forest Service workers as "pussies" for doing the work women can do, degrading their work by association. One fire fighter who was asked about the policy of affirmative action proclaimed, "It sucks." Especially in the logging communities they share, "we've got a bad enough name as it is," and bureaucratic initiatives to seek out women and minorities do not help. Another points out that loggers used to think of Forest Service workers as "a bunch of pansies, and now they've found out if they drive by and holler names at us, they get it right back, so they've changed their attitude." The change strikes him for the better, but he is presumably threatened by the presence of women. Interestingly, a woman says of passing loggers: "They used to go by a Forest Service pickup and give you the finger, but then they realized they were women, and they don't. Now they all honk and wave, and if you have a flat tire, they'll stop and help you or whatever you need."

This reflection of changing worker identity helps explain the passionate opposition of those men most on the defensive. The extreme military aura of the fire organization also militates against the presumably femininizing impact of women's gradual participation in fire fighting. Women just "take the fun out of fire camp" some feel, suggesting that the all-male and masculine atmosphere itself is what is at stake. Women may be acceptable in other field positions, but if they can fight fire too, where can the line be drawn? What will the difference be?

Male workers make their strongest stand against women in the context of fire fighting, and the grounds are lack of physical strength and endurance. The charge has very little to do with women's score on the step test and everything to do with their attitude toward their bodies, their work, and their co-workers. Some claim any man is stronger than any woman, thus women are physically disabled by sex alone. Others argue only that the typical female frame and musculature are typically less strong. Women, especially those without firsthand experience themselves, join in the critique. The woman fire fighter must be trying to "prove a point," the observer hears, and why? "She'd better be able to do as good a job as the man—she's taking his place. And to do that, you're going to have to look something like a young gorilla!"

On one point all agree. Like men, women improve with time with routine work or a regimen of conditioning exercises. A "new breed" of fire administrator, recognizing women's typical lifelong neglect of physique, suggests exercises for women interested in fire fighting, focusing on upper-body strength. And the exceptional woman is always acknowledged, if only grudgingly: "She was as good as—well, I guess she was better than some of the guys." Nearly every man has a story to tell about being outwalked, outworked, and generally outdone by a very strong woman.

Because women fire fighters can be observed working productively, the logic of the argument shifts to the boundaries of the routine. Can women work identically with men in style and result? Would an all-female crew be as productive as an all-male crew? When rappel crews walk miles out of a fire heavily laden with tools and supplies, who carries the extra weight of the 100-pound woman? Should a man be hit by a tree limb or falling rock during a forest fire, "is that woman going to be able to pick me up and carry me a mile?" When she goes "belly up" at the end of the day, who will do her job; and why should men on the line have to look out for her, jeopardizing their own safety?

Passing the step test convinces no one. The test itself reflects typical physical sex differences, although "the log's not going to squat down for a girl to go over." The real test is on the job and is virtually unpassable in the eyes of people convinced of male physical dominance. Rational arguments between women and men field workers break down at this point and tempers flare. Many times the issue reduces to personal challenge. The exchange reproduced below occurred during a human rights training session. To a woman's reminder that his crew included two highly successful women this year, a crew boss responded, "If I had the choice I wouldn't hire any of you." It's just "not where women belonged," he insisted. Then the challenge: "He said, 'Well, how about some day you and I go out and pack hose, both of us, up this hill, and see who gets there first.' And I said, 'Well, I'm not questioning the fact that you could probably get it there first. All I'm saying is, by God, I'll get it there, and I know other men who'd probably be behind *me*.'"

He was unconvinced, for incompetent men do not assuage his concern about incompetent women. The one-on-one challenge is usually a losing proposition for women, for the men who issue it value physical ability above all and speak from a position of strength. There is, as indicated below, no way under these terms for many women to qualify, and that is precisely the point: "One guy told me, 'When you throw me across your shoulder and carry me across the stream, I'll think about it. And then I'll throw *you* across my shoulder and *run* with you across the stream'—this kind of shit. That was how I had to qualify."

In the absence of other qualifications, sex alone can disqualify women, who are disabled by the association of strength and male physique. Through flimsy government office partitions one woman overheard her male co-worker complain of having "another damn woman" on his crew. When she objected, inquiring just exactly what made him feel as he did, he insisted that his feelings were only normal: "Well, there might have been somebody more qualified." To this she countered: "And how do you *know* that any *man* off that list might have weighed 300 pounds and would have had you rolling around the unit? You don't know that. You don't know anything more about a man than you do about a woman, and here you are, judging."

Sometimes the critique is appropriate. While prospective technicians in fire control are warned verbally of the rigors of the work, there is no teacher like experience. This woman's experience is not atypical:

> At first I was just astounded. I didn't have any idea, as far as fire was concerned. I had *no* idea what was happening, but it was a job, I was going to be outside, tooling up and down the mountains, I'd be in good physical health—oh, boy. I go there and—oh my goodness, to run into the problems I ran into as far as women being accepted. And then to get out there and find out—boy, I thought I was in pretty good physical health, and I am a disaster area!

Women and men alike find fire fighting a poor bargain, with poor working conditions and low wages, or simply discover themselves not equal to it; turnover can be as high as 50 percent in a season. For every woman who fails, all others face extra scrutiny, and most are careful, indeed eager, to acknowledge their limitations. While they feel capable and competent and find their strength growing daily, they quickly acknowledge weakness relative to their best male co-workers. This sentiment is widely shared: "I know that I'm not as strong as some men. I don't *try* to be. But I can do the job."

Women fire fighters and their supporters make many responses to the critics. They argue that the physical demands of the work are often exaggerated; the work is not impossibly difficult for an average adult in good condition. When the demand is extreme, it is shared; "killers" come rarely and are "heart-pounders" for everyone. The self-serving emphasis on the demands of work is very often misleading. This critic is describing off-season office work, but the point remains: "We do some work, and we smoke some dope, and we play some cards, and then we do some more work. I mean, it's not what you'd call a hard day. . . . and *they* go home and play 'Boy, did I have a hard day today' games with their wives. . . . And I was sitting there thinking, 'God, I know she worked harder with the six-month-old baby than *you* did today.'"

In a similar vein a woman accused of inadequacy describes the crews she knows best in arguing that fire fighting is not as strenuous as it is made out to be. Arriving at a lightning fire, the initial attack crew has two choices: "You get there and decide whether you're going to initial attack or whether you're going to smoke a joint first." On many crews hard-working women who are determined to prove themselves gain reputations as rate busters. Attitude and aptitude count too. "She may not be as capable of wielding a ten-pound sledge hammer, but at least she wields it," insists one supporter. Few male critics are impressed by the argument, for they are critical too of "lazy" or "laid-back" male workers who "make it look easy," thus encouraging women.

Supporters also argue that all workers are different and the differences between them are greater than those between the average man and woman. In fire as elsewhere there is always "a place for everybody," and as long as all are working and the job is completed correctly, work need not be identical here any more than it is on most other jobs. Does "fair share" mean proportionate effort or identical load, despite variations in conditioning, build, and experience? One crew boss who believes in identical loads deliberately overloads each woman "so she'll fall down or really have to struggle" and he can then lighten her load appropriately. Others object that equating "the Incredible Hulk" with the 110-pound worker actually forces failure; the crew boss is simply "putting her down in front of all those men—'you're not as good as us.'" Finally, what guarantee does any worker have that a partner, male or female, will be physically or psychologically able and willing to carry him or her to safety in an emergency? Testing of physical strength to stratify the labor force by increasingly fine cutoff points is "an endless process" and meaningless too.

Pace is important too, especially in fire situations where all workers must maintain a reserve of energy to help them out if necessary. The hare who sets too fast a pace is even less useful in the long run than the tortoise whose work is steady and dependable, concludes one experienced boss. Though very different in build, steady workers produce "a very similar amount of effort," and production standards have not dropped with the gradual employment of slightly smaller people. "If you set a good even pace and stay with it, that's a good day's work, and it's probably worth as much as the big bruiser that works in spurts." Speaking here of other field work, one woman on the permanent staff agrees:

When I go out there I can work all day, at my pace. . . . And I won't even attempt—you know, if I've got some guy out there trying to run me into the ground, just to see if I can take it. Well, you know—go ahead! Run ahead. I'll get there, don't worry about it. But I'm going at my pace. I can keep up with him for maybe half a day, but boy I'd really be beat at the end of the day if I were to keep that up all day. But there's nothing that says I have to go his pace. I'll get the job done.

When tasks are interdependent and pace becomes a negotiated issue, mutual adjustment is necessary: "I'll speed up and he can slow down." This is more difficult in pairs and less difficult in crew situations, where there is greater diversity of pace and the group tends to spread out. Some women also consciously compensate for slower pace by not taking lunch breaks or by working harder on other tasks. Slender fingers and limber bodies occasionally save the day too.

While women may not seem to get fully into the swing of things, sharing the bravado and enthusiasm of some workers, maybe it is just as well that they do not. Workers less prone to take risks are valuable too. Putting the point bluntly, one angry woman insists:

> *Anything* that can be done can be done by a woman, and it can probably be done better by a *sensible* woman out there, running the whole operation. You can hire a *monkey* to lift something or get a machine. They need people with good sense fighting fire. . . . Some guy said to me, "Hey, do you want to be a weeny?" And I said, "I don't get minus points for being a weeny." Women don't have to live up to the macho ethic, and the men do. . . . Guys get out there and they do crazy things. They're very unsafe. . . . She has no *reason* to get out there and be stupid in cowboy equipment, or throw hatchets at each other at lunch because it's cute, right?! They're going to say, "Hey, this is *dumb*."

Individual capacity and job motivation will continue to vary widely among workers. One parameter of variation will be sexual, just as factors like smoking, age, and conditioning influence general patterns of difference. What bearing, if any, these differences have on the long-term quality or quantity of the work at hand is impossible to establish systematically now. A host of factors intervene to influence job performance, from vegetation and terrain, weather, and the mix of personalities to financial incentives and career goals.

The recurring question of gender emerges again as the central issue in judging physical ability. Here too women face the old dilemma: how to be a competent worker without seeming to deny femininity or to imperil masculinity. "Vive la différence," the men testify again and again. The highly touted woman of exceptional ability is acceptable not because of her physical ability—indeed, she may downplay strength, skill, and experience—but in spite of it. Women new to the woods learn that few men actually expect comparable ability, nor (within limits) do they particularly like to see it. Small wonder management notes the pleasure some men take in being able to "carry" women's share. "Actually, I think they like it," one woman says of the day her blisters kept her indoors. "I think they really enjoyed seeing me in a bad way, and I was, too." The elusive "qualified" woman all approve is a figure far more complex than the "Amazon" or "young gorilla" or "macho woman" of organizational legend. The most successful newcomers to field work will recognize the physical challenge for the symbolic litmus test it is.

Ability and Disability

Women's perceived ability and attitude can be both enabling and disabling. Ironically, physical disability can be enabling and can facilitate women's integration, while objectionable attitudes effectively disable women from successful competition and entry. Men joke about the "anatomical handicap" large-breasted women face in field work, but behind the laughter is a model of women which is highly influential if rarely explicit—a model of women as in some way handicapped.

In the classic victim-blaming mode, women may be seen as hapless victims of circumstance, culturally deprived because "society failed to teach [them] how to use a hammer." The speaker continues: "You *know* it's not their fault. . . . [But I] can see why guys say 'I don't want a woman. Why don't you get a man, and I don't have to worry about it,' because he hasn't been culturally deprived."

Like other disabled persons women may seem to demand "special privileges" and conditions to facilitate unique needs—perhaps individual training in equipment maintenance or special consideration in language use in their presence. A woman may have been protected for years, and with her sudden entry into the "mainstream," her ignorance and naivete are highlighted. For some men, women at work pose problems of interaction as delicate as those involving the physically disabled.

Even more clear is the case of the woman whose legs are shorter, whose wind is less developed, or whose arms are unused to working a power saw for hours. Her condition or skill may improve, but forces also intervene to disable—weight gain, pregnancy, age, smoking, and so forth. There is a place for her nonetheless. After arguing that there are tasks at which all women are inferior to all men, one woman concludes: "There *are* jobs for everyone to do, like on a crew. And maybe you can't pick up half a log and throw it over there and throw it on the fire, but you can get somebody to help you do it. And if you've got somebody who's got like a bad back, or a wooden leg, there's lots of jobs they can do without doing that."

Of the young disabled field worker just hired, an observer notes with approval: "That gal can do anything—I'm not kidding. She works that stump like you wouldn't believe." In the same spirit women field workers are encouraged, despite their limitations of sex or size or conditioning.

The task is made easier by compensatory development of strengths, both for the physically disabled and for women. Very often women freely acknowledge ways in which they feel less capable and effective than the men around them but note the strengths they feel they bring to the job. These relative strengths and weaknesses emerge in the informal division of labor within crews as well as in larger patterns of segregation. Women pride themselves on their skill on the typewriter or adding machine, or on the habitual extra effort they put into their work, for instance. For some, inferiority in one realm is made easier to accept because "usually a woman is better in something else, whether it's figures or printing or keeping tallies or something like detail work." This skill in turn compensates for their inadequacy as men, whose place on the crew they feel they fill.

Accepting inadequacy is important. No matter how capable, the wrong-minded worker has a troubled future. Conveying an "attitude" can be physically threatening in some woods jobs too, as suggested by the woman who complains of suspicious field accidents, and by the woman who made the following statement:

> You don't want to go in there, because the tests that they put you through and the situations they put you into—your life is on the line all the time. And you do *not* need to have some guy pulling a head trip on you when you're about to get your rear end scorched. That's the last thing you need. "Hey, it's like this, folks—I'm not out here to prove a point. I enjoy being outside. I enjoy doing the type of work. And I'm *not* trying to take a job away from you or prove I can do it better than you. You're stronger than me, there's no doubt in my mind! Don't do this to me! Jimminy Christmas, back off, for heaven's sake!"

Whether through prior sex-role training, physical limitations, or attitude, women new to field work can be seen as handicapped in some elementary and irrefutable way. Their presumed deformity may also determine how men act toward them. But handicap and difference must be visible. The case of mistaken identity occurs frequently in these accounts and is always vividly recalled.

Men in the woods are caught off balance by women appearing incognito, indistinguishable from men because of dress or activity or company. Some field women are charged with overcompensating in an effort to disguise their sex (women "passing" as normals?). Others self-consciously display such telltale signs as earrings, wedding rings, or hair clasps.

There is always room for misunderstanding, as the following story of a woman working with contractors suggests:

> The Forest Service didn't know quite how the crews out there would react to me. And so I just marched out there. But of course I was dressed in pants and shirt and a hat, and until I spoke, nobody knew. [One "real nice feller" demonstrating a technique registered real shock when she spoke up to ask for information.] He looked up at me and said, "You're a woman!" "Oh, I hope so!" "Oh my, I must tell the fellows." "Why?" "Well, there's just things . . . that happen out here. They need to know there's a woman around." ["Come to find out," the problem was the men's habit of peeing from the top of their rigs.]

Like people who are disabled, women in the field work with special visibility and under special conditions. As a special category of worker, there is a place for them—but not for too many of them. Those first few women to get jobs with the Forest Service outdoors laugh at the dismay with which they felt they were greeted—"what do we do with *two* of 'em?" The analogy is limited, of course, if suggestive. Enabling and debilitating qualities are not always obvious. A physical or social handicap can be endearing; only defects of attitude and stance truly cripple women's efforts to gain acceptance.

The Protection Racket

Many dimensions of ability and attitude come in for inspection during this early phase of worker integration, from the newcomer's skill and experience to her appearance, politics, or religiosity. In addition, her sense of herself as a woman is at issue. Feelings about both feminism and femininity emerge in the face of a male tendency toward protectiveness and female assertion of competence.

For women the task is to demonstrate ability without giving offense.[4] One of the principal ways these tricky waters are negotiated is through the proffering and acceptance of male help. While an ethic of common courtesy in the woods prevails (e.g., holding the branches back for the next person), not all workers or crews share a common inclination to help each other out concretely. The feeling is widespread that no one should be allowed to struggle with his or her work, but one crew may sit on the slope and enjoy a cup of coffee as the stragglers finish, while nearby nobody stops work until all are done and can share in the coffee break. There is more latitude for help in some jobs than others, where all

workers have discrete tasks. Some individuals do not routinely go out of
their way to help others; some help women and men alike, and some will
help only women. Many report they help women more, usually because it
"comes naturally" or is "built into" them; one old-timer observes, however, that before offering help they will "give 'em a fair chance to fail."
Help is rarely so easily offered to other men, who may take offense:
"Come on, buddy—I'll get it done!"

In integrated situations, routine courtesies in field work merge with a
kind of chivalry, as some men offer to carry backpacks or tools even when
weighted with their own, rush to get to doors first despite heavy loads or
full hands, or automatically take the more difficult units or tools to work
with. Sometimes this behavior comes under the rubric of "respect" and is
precisely what some women expect. To them it seems nicer, more feminine in fact, to accept these small courtesies graciously and defer to a
male desire to please, however archaic it may seem. Others find the
men's conduct exceedingly strange.

Men often agree that this help offered and accepted is more symbolic
than genuinely needed. Small gallantries come easily and can be independent of on-the-job interaction. Women may pull their own weight as
one of the crews, but "just the same, when you get back to the office, nine
out of ten times the same crew member you worked shoulder to shoulder
with cutting brush will open the door for you," one woman happily
reports. The woman who worked hard all day next to her partner was
floored when one weekend he spoke sternly to her about not continuing
to carry out the (fairly large and heavy) bunkhouse garbage can; while
his behavior was mysterious to her, she was happy to comply, if only to
please him.

The sexual politics of help color small and large moments of interaction. One woman recalls the day she and another woman hoisted bags of
fertilizer in the back while her older male partner drove the truck. They
suddenly became giggly and could no longer even begin to lift heavy
weights. At this moment a log truck slowly passed as the driver stared
incredulously at the women struggling in the back while the Forest
Service man sat in the driver's seat. "He really balled him out for not
helping us," she remembers; the driver had deeply offended their partner with the insinuation of unmanliness.

The most clear-cut instance usually occurs away from home during
major forest fires beyond local resources. There women on the fire line
move in an atmosphere almost exclusively male, one of a few women in
hundreds, perhaps thousands, of men. These fire fighters may include
contract crews (including convict crews) and Forest Service workers from
around the country unfamiliar with the sight, more common in the

Northwest, of women at camp in nontraditional roles (e.g., serving as time keepers, supply clerks, drivers). Strange men from around the country mingle with the more familiar faces from a woman's own and nearby districts. There will be "hoots and hollers" when she is noticed, perhaps catcalls too, and often a general amazement or vague hostility. In this setting more than one woman has experienced some degree of intimidation. After forcibly holding closed the toilet door against a deter- mined stranger (sexual labels of the portable toilets were promptly dis- regarded), one woman happily accepted male co-workers' offers to accompany her to the bathroom. Another story is similar:

> If some woman went off by herself . . . , women on one crew went off, and the men from another crew started giving them a really bad time and really went after them—that crew was there, real quick. It was kind of amazing! . . . I guess I went over to the shower rooms, and I was coming back (it was a quarter mile on the trail) and I was just about back to camp, and a whole crew of men came out. They were just giving me a real hard time, about going over to the shower room, not having any business there. And it was really strange because they had women on their crew too, and I had just left them in the showers! They were just real irate, and they'd been drink- ing. . . . No, it wasn't real comfortable. I was definitely outnumbered!

Again her own crew members were fast upon the scene, and rarely was she alone again. As one district ranger put it, in this situation male protectiveness just seems to come naturally, "like dominant males in an animal group." At any rate, women at fire camp are happily defended by co-workers: "I don't care what the atmosphere is at home, but when they go someplace they're a full member of the group. . . . You don't mess around with the girls in another crew," notes one supervisor. Perhaps such situations are less likely as more fire crews are integrated; for the present, women in this situation are generally pleased to accept this attention and protection. In their particularly vulnerable position it strikes them as natural too.

At other times the inclination to protect out-of-place women comes as more of a surprise and is taken as an unwarranted intrusion. "The only time I feel incompetent," one experienced field worker insists, is when men insist on doing work for her. The limiting nature of protectiveness is evident. In an extreme case a professional woman's supervisor consis- tently refused her request to drive to and from the field or to work independently, citing fear for her safety. At the end of the season she was outraged when he downgraded her for lack of independent work. Men and women see this matter very differently. The man who left a woman in camp during a fire and faced her subsequent formal complaint objects: "She said that we were discriminating against her, but actually what we were trying to do was to *take care of her* and the crew."

The impulse to protection is largely situational. It is also more likely among strangers, and during particularly dirty, demanding, or risky work, and is more predictable from older men. Unnecessary help may be tolerated out of respect for older men with traditional backgrounds, whose gallantry seems impossible to challenge effectively. The situation described below is not uncommon:

> I got all my crew straightened out, and someone new would come on, and do things like give me their hand to help me up hills. When I went to [the new district] my boss was fifty-six years old, and he really wanted to baby me. You know, he had me on a pedestal—it was the whole bit. And I could never change him, especially where he was coming from. . . . I *didn't* deal with him—I let him protect me, you know.

Some men "just feel real bad" at the sight of women climbing down steep gorges and fighting their way through dense brush; to them, protecting women is a matter of manners. It is also often transitional, even fleeting. This woman recalls her first days as the only woman on an all-male brush crew: "When we walked out of the crummy, one guy asked me if I'd like him to carry my axe! I said 'No, I think I can carry my own axe.' They were pretty nice to me at first, and treated me like a lady, at *first*. And then they realized—well, I was just one of the guys after a bit, and they realized they didn't have to be real nice to me."

The protective attitude assumes various forms. Particularly strong or experienced men often convey this feeling to all those around them regardless of sex, just as some bosses create a more conservative, risk-avoiding climate for their crew. Protectiveness is often suggestive of traditional family relations, and for women that model is both familiar and oppressive. Frequently they report that "the guys considered me as their little sister, and they watched out, protected me." One reports how she was carefully trained to use the chain saw, but then "in the beginning, I was always fighting to be able to use it."

> They were real protective of me, you know. And I think that happens a lot with men, whether they realize it or not, whether they've been saying, "Aw, you can handle it—go out and do your own". . . . When it comes down to it, they're real, real protective of who you are—which is a real nice feeling at the same time. If it wasn't so fatherly, it'd be a lot nicer—you know, if it was more compadre. . . . But I think that even happens too.

This paternalistic form of the protection racket embodies implicit assumptions about appropriate relationships; fathers dominate and discipline daughters, just as they offer protection. How easily well-intentioned guidance and assistance become patronizing, undermining a sense of competence and autonomy. The following anecdote illustrates the paternal mode and suggests its intangible and apparently benign quality, which makes effective rejoinder or resistance so difficult. The speaker is a young, fairly conservative woman rather new to outdoor work, in excellent physical condition and independently minded. She tells the story of the first time she went by herself to get the rig the crew had left on the road above. To save walking time for all, someone would necessarily return to the rig and would meet the others below. The men were skeptical when she volunteered, but she persisted, pointing to her compass and assuring them she knew where the rig was parked.

> So John says "All right, you can do it." Then he looked at me and said, "But you have new boots and I want you to be really careful out there. I want you to think about that. I know you've been jumping around the logs and everything today with us, but now you're going by yourself, and you have to think about these new boots." It was really funny. Like, I was going to break my legs out there with my *new boots* on!

When she met them with the truck later on, she arrived in good spirits: "I always get this really good feeling, like I look at them, like 'Aha! I did it, see?' And they always say [in a tone familiar to obedient dogs], 'Very good. You did a good job, good job.'"

While some women find this concern comforting and comfortable, by and large they try to avoid it. They are very sensitive to the protection trap and its potential effect on their career and relations with men at work in the long run. They recognize the interaction of testing, proving, and protecting: "I think it was more of a testing of what I was willing to do and what I wanted to do. I think if I would have let them protect me . . . like I think that can easily happen. If you let them do that, they'll pigeon-hole you, and I think that if I would have let them get away with that, I'd have spent all my time in the office."

It is humanly tempting to take advantage of small favors freely offered, and most workers would welcome an extra cup of coffee, a hike unburdened by an extra few pounds, or the warmth of the cab while others scramble to fix flat tires. But to accept male protection is risky. Many agree that, like elephants, men have long memories: "But I feel that's something that really affects the view of women working in the field, for women to allow the men to do that. Because then the men will turn around and say that you're not carrying the burden—'you're not doing your share'—which *is* real true."

Field-going women are painfully aware of the dilemma and ambivalent about their response. Some feel genuinely compelled on principle to participate wholeheartedly at all times, as one "taking the place on the crew of a man," while others are happy with their more qualified role. Uncertainty for some is flexibility for others: "I've got such an advantage over everyone else here. They know I can do it, but they don't expect me to do it. They don't demand that I do it. If I do, fine. If I don't, fine." This is precisely the dual set of expectations others are determined to avoid. But how far to take it? "I have had that feeling [male protectiveness] several times on other [than fire] jobs—to just have something taken right out of my hands. I hate that feeling, I just hate it! Then sometimes it's fine with me. I mean, if they want to break their back to prove something, I really don't care *that* much."

While some men may be concerned to outperform all others, the woman quoted below and many like her feel no impulse to cultivate a reputation for derring-do but wonder if they should: "A lot of times I would think, 'You should do it. You should get in there—show them you can handle it.' But then I thought, to hell with that. That's the same game they're playing. And I know I can handle it if I had to do it. And if they *want* to do it, let them go ahead and do it. . . . I'm not particularly into risking my life."

These feelings complicate the dilemma women in the field confront. The task is to parry gestures of male protection without giving offense and without compromising their own sense of ability and pride. Portraits of popular and unpopular women illustrate the contradiction between abstract qualities and acceptance in practice. For example, men clearly reject women who "use their femininity," though many enjoy playful co-workers more than serious women disinclined to indulge chivalrous pleasantries. Male workers and bosses demand competence from incoming women but rarely care to see excellence or competitive ability actively demonstrated. Ability must be conveyed without impugning masculinity or femininity. Uncompromising insistence upon independence makes weaker workers burdensome to all and is a wellspring of the subsequent denial of any help—the "Gloria Steinem" treatment some women face.

To many men, rejection of assistance is a political statement. A cartoonist captures this sentiment in sketching a woman hanging on for dear life over a looming precipice; a man running up hollers, "Are you a feminist, or would you like some help?" Women resentful of help are "those on the macho trip—the ERA thing," that is, not the "ladylike" but the feminist women. Those who refuse (however nicely) this special relationship may be denied common courtesy as well. Few are as adamant as this man, angered by women who refuse doors held open for them: "I'll only do it once. If somebody gives me a bad time, next time they'll be knocked down."

> [If] you're putting on an act to be that way, to try to be accepted, it doesn't work. It's one of the worst things you can do! But if you're basically a lady, and you want to go into a field like this, pull our own weight and do what you should do, but still be a lady, you can do it. . . . They'll accept that faster than anything. As long as you do your work, do your share and don't scrimpinize on it—like not digging line, just walking up the line—or being a women's libber and telling 'em, proving 'em, that you—"I can be just as good as you or better." They'll just turn you off faster than anything. Just sort of still have that lady atmosphere about you . . . and you can be accepted, no problem, and be considered one of the guys.

That "lady atmosphere" seems imcompatible with feminist politics. Part of the "mellow" image is learning not to take offense easily, and a kind of competitive tolerance emerges as women draw lines at different points. Small matters can loom large. Being called a woman and not a girl is important to some, while others resist only direct job actions against them or other women.

Some women too equate femininity with deference to male help, and define feminism as the ostentatiously "libby" assertion of independence. Thus one woman wonders that anyone might take offense at the tiniest little special favors men at work proffer: "I'm feminine enough to enjoy that special attention." For others the acceptance of help, necessary or not, is a kind of gesture of appeasement, a small price to pay to keep things calm. Most try not to "rub the edges raw" by insisting on their independence and competence, and only a few cannot accept some degree of male help.

Feminist women seen as "harping" or "crusading" are easy targets for men who don't want their "face rubbed into it all the time." Managers regret the occasional militants who reflect poorly on affirmative action programs and "do themselves a disservice" with their defensive attitude. Like "pushy" blacks, outspoken feminists are "not very popular with most men"; their feminist talk is no more palatable, one manager notes, than the language of black power. The feminist focus detracts from the dynamic of blending in, as this long-time administrator suggests. If matters were only so simple: "If you want equality, I guess . . . , act the role. Just *be* equal. Don't *make* differences—don't preach EEO, for example. . . . Just do it, go out and do the job and don't ask for special favors, and you won't have any problems."

All the races up steep hillsides, the jokes about deteriorating language and filthy bodies, and the carefully cultivated opportunities for chivalry in the woods indicate the same thing: the eventual discovery of a comfortable way of relating, so necessary to these groups working intimately in remote places. The protection racket described here helps mediate the contradictions women woods workers feel and is in any case difficult to refuse gracefully. Deference to male protection is more likely in the beginning, when all else is also uncertain and strengths and weaknesses not yet established. It is an important part of the undercurrent of interaction during women's integration into woods work.

Models of Accommodation

In the Forest Service, indoor and outdoor work and workers are jumbled. Activity moves inside and outside with the cycle of work and season; daily weather, promotion, and occasional job detail bring workers to more and less physical work. Various models of social relations coexist and occasionally directly confict. Women may meet men as buddies in the woods, as workers "*totally* female" in the office, and perhaps as sexual partners after work. The intimacy of office and community can put workers in uneasy contact; women meet supervisors as well as unfamiliar men at the downtown bar when there is only one. One woman was keenly aware of the limits to her acceptance: "But you want to know something funny? After work, when we're partying, they treated me as a *girl*. I never was allowed to enter in on what-happened-at-work talk."

The juxtaposition of traditional and nontraditional, office and field women, dressed-up and dressed-down field women, on-work and off-work relations, all intensify uncertainty in new models of relations between the sexes. Developing a model of accommodation that works is essential to women's integration as workers and as women: "If you present yourself all along the way you want to be treated, that's the way you'll be treated. And I firmly believe in that. The guys are very easy to work with, and will treat you like what you want to be treated like. And I have seen gals who have . . . gotten just what they asked for!"

Women learn what to do and how to be by watching what happens to those who go against the grain. By reacting, interacting, and sometimes overacting, they find the modes of relating that work best in various contexts. They discover, some sooner than others and some few not at all, what kind of woman men want to work with. Most feel it right that as newcomers they do their best to measure up. The persona operates principally to help women "fit in nicely" in their immediate situation.

These models are not mutually exclusive or fixed in time and space. They are fundamentally interactive ways of being, shaped and reshaped as women learn more about the particular men around them. From their descriptions of troublesome women, helpful hints to newcomers, and thumbnail self-portraits, a number of these models of accommodation can be described.[5]

Some of these models are rooted in the familiar territory of family relations. Asked if she felt like "one of the guys," one woman spoke as if to clear up a misunderstanding: "Well, I don't have to act like I'm a guy—I'm the old lady and the grandmother part of it. . . . Mom, you know." This style is familiar, generally threatening, and unambiguous. Grandmotherly women in the field are not competitive; mothers urge warm clothes and safety and are available for advice on matters of health or personal problems. Women adopting this model may be ignored, but rarely are they antagonists; they are irrelevant.

Very often women describe co-workers as brothers, and (more rarely) men describe women as sisters, in an easy transposition of asexual relations from the realm of the family to the family at work. Little sisters tend to have lots of "big brothers" affording a degree of protective custody. Ostensibly a model egalitarian relationship, the brotherly-sisterly mode is misleadingly benign. In work, as in the family, stereotypic relations prevail, and the sociological future of the sister is quite different from that of her brother.

The flirt or pet is a popular style, building on sexual tensions in relations at work that many find intriguing. Flirts easily become group mascots and a source of "ego support" and "merriness" to men. Their role is carefully circumscribed, for they amuse the group at the pleasure of those men who enjoy them. The flirt or lover is a potentially powerful figure whose future as a legitimate co-worker is constrained. The pet is even more clearly irrelevant, as one angry woman knows and tries to explain to a younger woman:

> They may *like* you and think you are cute and treat you like a pet, but goddamn it, they'll never promote you. They hate my guts! They might not like it, but if they have to, they'll give me the responsibility in a pinch. They wouldn't give it to her on a bet. . . . They may hate me, but they know I've got the skill. I'm capable. She's got the disadvantage. . . . she'll be their token, their pet, their cutey-pie. . . . She thinks they "really, really like her."

Other women rely on roles structured around confessional disability or handicap (eagerly admitting limitations), self-concept as foreigner or tyro (always learning and eager to be taught), or vivid physical competence (the "Amazon," a nonthreatening freak). Though few consciously adopt the style, the "women's libber" is a familiar model tolerated with bemused inattention if she is amusing. Alternative models are explored and familiar ones fine-tuned. A woman entering the workplace quite content to play the flirt may desperately rely on the handicap dynamic to manage her remaining days on the crew. The "little sister" may be radicalized through confrontation and may be converted to a more overtly feminist model. The inevitable changes always surprise. When the "great little grandmother figure stood up and said 'screw you in the shorts,'" both female and male co-workers were stunned. Every woman who values her male "buddies" also knows the casual ways of flirtation and the elements of other models too. Dynamic and multidimensional, models of accommodation vary in intensity and intent and mean different things to different people. At their heart these models are fundamentally defined and enforced not by women but by men.

The degree of conformity women can muster with these preferred models is an important indicator of successful accommodation. This is also true for male newcomers. As a pastor, one young man imposed an unwelcome restraint on the atmosphere of the group and paid the penalty. Another concluded he simply "didn't drink enough beer" (and was too highbrow) ever really to fit in with the other men. The structure of work places inordinate emphasis on compatibility, on getting and going along. Women and men are rewarded for their conformity with preferred styles of interaction and relative ability to modulate personal style and demeanor appropriately.

Femininity and the Ladylike Buddy

For women, the baseline questions are: What do you really expect? What are you out here for? Do you want to be treated like a man or a woman? In fact, women's feelings are irrelevant, as men continue both to ask and to answer the question. They prefer women co-workers who are at once a part of and apart from the masculine ways at work, who blend in yet always stand apart. Like this woman, most try to "fit just enough": "I try to fit just enough into each person. . . . that's how I always do it. And I feel bad that I had to compromise so much, because I should be able to do exactly what I want to—either be very feminine or very . . . athletic. But I found it was just easier, to break in gently."

Neither the "Little Miss routine" nor "pretending to be something she's not" are acceptable, hence the importance of learning to strike the right balance and "break in gently." Femininity and deference, for example, can be situational, even calculating, and still satisfy:

> Like, you're one of the guys and you can accept them as they are and they accept you as you are, in the sense that you can go along and tell them dirty jokes and stuff. . . . But yet you're still . . . feminine, in a way that you sort of *act* feminine. Like if they offer to do something, like cut the root for you or open the door, you don't [shout], "No, I can do it!" You just sort of [sweetly], "Sure, go ahead." Thank them for it and everything. . . . You've got to sort of know *when* to just be one of the guys.

One woman insists, "They won't allow you—they won't allow your femininity to *not* be maintained." They expect competence but not competition, and limitations rather than capabilities: "They were glad I tried, but they didn't even really expect me to. I was surprised. . . . I don't even think they wanted me to. You know, they don't want me to be something I'm not."

One of the clearest dangers is "overdoing it," essentially overacting. Competitive behavior and a "manlike" appearance must be avoided. Field-going women don't "slop around a bunch of profanity just to fit in." Dress must be conservative, though a woman must not "look like a sack of potatoes" or go too far toward disguising sexuality. Remembering forestry school, this woman stresses being "Suzy Comfortable"—affecting neither the clothes of the logger nor those of "Suzy Co-ed": "But not wearing the men's . . . I mean, in other words, the first step is to fall right into the men's world. I mean, right down to how much wood you can chop. . . . And there are still a lot of women who are still going through that transition."

Her point is important, for it is a transition. Women in the woods will be roundly criticized whenever they overstep the boundary, however, and they generally accept the point.

Concretely, what does it mean to blend in as a female buddy? It means sharing an intimacy bounded by work: "You're a buddy, on the work basis. . . . You're not a supervisor or someone you work with. You know 'em deeper than that because you spend eight hours a day doing one task together, which means you're both sliding down cliffs and trying to pick up the pieces of each other or supporting each other in the bad situations—'catch me when I fall!'"

In the best case, it means "being as natural around them as they can be around me" or simply being "one of their friends—I work with them, I drink with them, I sleep with some of them." It may also involve a physically different relationship: "They want to start treating you like one of the guys . . . , smack you on the back or rough you up, to where I don't think they would think about doing it to a woman in the office." It means learning to "take it" like the "good sport" a woman should be. Like ethnics hearing ethnic jokes, women should take jokes and comments about women in stride. Conversational conformity may be expected too: "[She] can really pitch in to men's conversations, because she fishes and talks about chain saws and all that stuff, but I don't—and that's what they expect you to do. They don't expect you to start talking about world politics or something that they don't want to talk about. 'If you come into *my* world, talk about what we want to talk about.'"

Being "one of the guys" comes easily for some and incompletely and uncertainly for others; in any event, it takes time. Each new woman desegregating a department or crew experiences the process anew. This story illustrates clearly the evolving sense of segregation and integration as the outsider becomes an insider:

> Well, when I first got on the crew, they weren't quite sure how to take it— "Oh gee, here's a female—we've got to clean up our language!" You know, this sort of thing. . . . They played it fairly straight for one day until they heard me swearing a blue streak as I was crashing through the brush and being really obnoxious about the whole thing, and they decided "Oh, she's one of us!" It took them about two days to decide that I was one of the guys. . . . I've had an awful lot of jobs where I've been working in a pretty much predominantly male field. And the guys will at first usually try to be a little bit different, you know, and they start treating you as . . . a "lady" or whatever. And then after a few days you get to be one of the guys and things are different. And then if another female comes in they start acting like "uh, oh, here's a female. . . . we've got to clean up our act again," and they expect *me* to clean up my act too. That's what's funny! It's like I'm one of the guys and therefore I've got to go along with it. . . . I've got to shape up again—no dirty jokes, no off-color language. I get such a kick out of it!

Some find this intimacy precious, but to others it comes perilously close to abandoning femininity in the search for male approval. Knowing they "can't expect to be *real* feminine" in their daily work, must they risk "giving up" femininity altogether because they prefer outdoor work? Can one of the guys be a lady too? A number of women worry about compromising too much, aware they "pick up habits I don't particularly care to have" when they drink and swear and relax with their new buddies at work.

The young woman working with an engineer intent on training and encouraging her professionally, while also expounding on the sexual "notches on his belt," summed up the problem: "It didn't occur to him in one area that I was a woman, and then in another area it didn't occur to him that I was a woman!" Another woman wonders if she asks too much; her own feelings are muddled and new:

> There were lots of times when I *wanted* to be respected as a woman out there. . . . There's a lot of things when you're working with men in the woods that you don't want to hear, you know? Men together kind of . . . I don't know, sometimes they end up talking and joking about things that are directly related to women that I really don't want to hear. . . . So at the time you kind of have to . . . set up differences. So it's real difficult. You don't want to be treated as someone different, but then you really want respect. And lots of times that will be thrown at you—"Here you are, working with us. . . . well, you're going to listen to this."

Women are exhorted "not to make a big thing of the differences." Managers and others urge them "not to dress in a way that would cause the men to be attracted"—rarely a real issue in field garb. Many women testify to their determination to "put the male-female distinction thing away when I'm working." Few women, and fewer men, sense that this deemphasis on sexuality can be a loss. One male co-worker echoes the complaint of "not getting laid" upriver in a small Forest Service community; a woman living upriver, however, puts the issue differently: "Yeah, it really does work. They *do* accept you. But if you ever wanted to change that role to be. . . . A woman like that has a hard time finding a lover. You know, she is a 'good old boy.' She does not require . . . nurturing and orgasms. It's a rare woman that gets both."

Occasionally field workers argue that to be one of the crew is not necessarily to be one of the guys. Yet most men and women define "the brotherhood" at work in traditional masculine terms, though some argue that the ambience ("crude and lewd") resides in woods work and is irrelevant to masculinity or femininity. A slip of the tongue is revealing. Women who work well generally fit right in, one man insists, and they are "treated as men—as fellow workers." Most agree that femininity and masculinity are implicated in the sexual integration of woods work. They worry about women field workers becoming "totally equal—to get rid of *all* the femininity," as if femininity were the principal stumbling block to male acceptance.

Differences are important, especially to men who find masculinity and femininity and the differences between them pleasurable and rewarding. A most supportive man spoke to this issue. An avid ball player, he very nearly lost his temper speaking of plans to integrate his league sexually. The game is "one of the few things they've *got* to keep stratified," for what else is there? "Like the Wednesday night guys' poker game—isn't there any more privacy to do what you want to do?" Accustomed to change at work, he keenly resents the lack of respect for sexual barriers in other parts of his life. Preserving male camaraderie against female insurgency is important to the male effort to control female entry in woods work. Other men may not share the commitment to single-sex sports, but his wholehearted defense of boundaries, limits, and a decent interval between the sexes strikes home.

Women working with men share some of these feelings, though they put a different light on the question. They want very much to "try and fit in and yet not lose—not let them try to make a man out of you . . . and not try to use being a female either. A hard line to walk!" Some know all too well how close they walk to failure—to overcompensating, or not measuring up, or both. And they can never be certain: "I'd like to hear what the guys have to say about it. I go out and I push to be able to do the same things, and they *seem* to accept it, and they accept me. And they seem to accept me being feminine even though I am . . . doing the same thing they're doing."

Field-working women are sensitive to their claims to femininity. The litany of traditional feminine characteristics—real women are sweet-smelling, long-haired, clean and good-looking—comes easily to the men at work, and the contrast between field and office women is always evident. Some of the men who work with them find them unfeminine and unattractive; they may not be in the "having-to-help category" of women, but neither are they candidates for a date, and they know it. To some this is just as well, for it helps defuse the sexual tension in the air, but for others it is painful. Even those rejecting traditional indicators of womanliness (as most do) acknowledge the importance of the question of femininity. Many feel that constant association with men, especially in this outdoor atmosphere, raises the danger of masculinization. It seems somehow to rub off and must be guarded against, and femininity must be protected. Some compensate by taking advantage of opportunities to wear skirts or dresses when appropriate, using less obscene language off work, and other tactics. Like many in her situation, the young woman quoted below is very sensitive to this dilemma and is happy to report being treated as someone special:

> It's been kind of encouraging too, because there *is* a different way that I'm treated than the guys. You know, it's really subtle. But I'm always aware that I'm a woman. And it's kind of nice to be hot and sweaty and filthy dirty and straining with everybody else—just sort of the opposite of what the culture gives you as standards of femininity, you know, pretty and clean, nice and

cutesy. And here I am just the opposite and I'll still feel very feminine. The guys will still treat me as being special. They make me feel that I'm pretty and that I'm nice and that I'm accepted regardless of what I look like.

For others, it is important too but comes much harder:

> It does bother me quite a bit at times—what they think as far as . . . femininity. In fact, I will use those situations that arise to show that I'm really a girl. Like if we have some sort of a dinner or something, I'll wear a dress, just to throw them off a little and remind them I'm a girl. . . . Sometimes you're just out there *so ugly* and filthy and just—you're just gross looking and you know it. And you feel just awful. You just really want to tell them you're a girl, you can be pretty sometimes. But it's kind of hard out there. You usually have to do it after work or something.

Competence in traditionally male jobs threatens to contradict claims to femininity.[6] The good friend of a woman just joining the elite air operations in the fire organization (previously dominated by Vietnam veterans and with a regionwide reputation for true grit) counsels her to cultivate the trappings of femininity carefully. Wear a scarf, she urges, or take in some brownies occasionally; perhaps even wear a flower in your hair once in a while. It is important to "not let them make you manlike. Don't let them use that for an excuse, the reason why you can do just as good as they can." In jobs less endowed with feminine or masculine qualities, this "acting the part" (for example, as the "lady fire fighter") may be less necessary.

Others judge femininity more a matter of mental attitude. They are more critical of the woman who always tries to compete and excel or who develops an "overcompensating" demeanor (e.g., affecting "cigars and a welding hat") than they are of those who are "still a woman" and whose sweaty bodies are only natural indicators of a full day's work in the woods. Femininity is clearly not confined to appearance, though no definition strays far from this baseline. No one in this organization confuses men with women or women with men, no matter how black they may be at the end of a long shift on the fire line. Some women field workers may take their handwork along during the long rides to the job site or may bring baked goods from home to share at noon. The "woman's touch" is recognized for what it is. One district office now has plants and pictures creating a "homier" feeling, and the young woman responsible notes that it is appreciated: "It's like—*they* couldn't have done it, but they're glad it was done. There's a lot of things like that that I do, or try to do, that I know they wouldn't do if it was up to them. Either it would offend their masculinity, or . . . It took them so long to admit to anybody that they bring salads in their lunch—something so minor!"

Quite another matter, all agree, is the woman who attempts to evade work through "playing on her femininity." While the prevailing feeling is that this behavior is out of bounds, too many women have observed men in action around particularly attractive or flirtatious women to take their principled objections at face value. "Feminine wiles" are purportedly dysfunctional at work, but like "bees to honey," men seem to cluster around the desk of the newest attractive woman. They conscientiously allow less glamorous women to carry their full share of heavy loads but are quick to offer help to gorgeous new women entering the scene. The attractive woman with "nothing but big brothers" is also a familiar figure:

> And I've seen women that I would have liked to kick their butts in, because I've seen the position where there were women like me down in the fire, working on the fire, and there was this cute little blonde with the earrings and clean clothes sitting on top, because her *male* fire crew thought it was so cute that she could sit up there and do *nothing!* It can go either way—they'll work your butt off, or they'll slide the other way.

A woman does not have to be the "super-dainty, good-looking, Play-boy-centerfold type" men reportedly "fall all over themselves to do work for" in order to be appreciated as a feminizing and (some say) humanizing force at work. There are many reasons why women in the field are seen as a positive force by some men. Others agree with the experienced technician who finds that "it gets pretty darn hard-core out there," and with women around, the "push, push, push, shove" atmosphere is somewhat relaxed. Women are seen as a civilizing force by this man's wife as well. She was slow to come to grips with her jealousy when he began working closely with younger women, but now she makes the following point: "It's a lot better at home too . . . , not having to gear up for home life, after being out there in the jungle, so to speak, and the language and stuff like that—having to regear, coming home talking to kids and to a wife."

Clearly femininity transcends conformity to prevailing sex-role expectations and engages far more than physical appearance. The dichotomy between the "ladylike" field worker and the "macho woman" parallels that of the feminine and the feminist, drawing more on the realm of demeanor and attitude than on that of ability or appearance. It is intimately linked to sexuality and centrally engages the concept of deference. Essentially situational and emergent, the precious sense of personally and culturally valid femininity is as elusive as it is integral to personality and social interaction. If only obscurely, it colors many moments of interaction in the woods.

After earlier asserting that all the difficult problems raised by female field workers had long since been resolved, one man stumbled when it came to defining what made women in the field feminine, with their foul language and sweaty bodies, and explaining how they were at once one of the guys and ladies too. As he concluded, "The answers—they're not all there for all these questions."

This ambiguity and uncertainty is the most important point. Neither women nor men are of one mind about the proper relationship between sexuality and work or about the most effective model of accommodation. It is a puzzling time. Many women—and some men—are rethinking what femininity and masculinity imply and what they want from work. Though she wants to be "accepted as myself," one thoughtful woman is not so sure what that acceptance means: "I've probably tried to be one of the boys, which is a good way to get the work done but it is not good for myself. . . . Because I lose half myself. I lose the feminine part of myself. . . . Anyway, I would like to see women working in the woods and men accepting how we would work in the woods, as women."

Summary

This chapter considered the pressures of visibility on women field workers and some of their responses. Two dimensions of this special vulnerability emerged as particularly important during the early phase of testing and proving.

The concept of the protection racket illustrates the difficult position of women, for they are challenged to demonstrate competence and also to affirm male superiority. The interaction of gender and ability complicates women's sense of femininity and also shapes the on-going definition of feminism. Continued deference to male gestures of chivalry in the woods is a solution many women reject because of the long-term consequences of the protection racket for their reputation and careers.

No challenge to women's physical ability is more extreme than fire fighting. The masculine nature of project fire camps makes them particularly difficult. Male opposition to women in fire is ideologically grounded in physical prowess but is linked also to the defense of valued work and worker reputation, for the prospect of women feminizing the workplace is threatening.

Women's attitude transcends their ability in successful entry. Various models of accommodation ease the acceptance of women. In particular, the ladylike buddy model suggests a balance for the newcomers between blending in and standing out. While largely effective, the search for acceptance is not without cost, and some workers question its long-term impact on women and their work.

5

Sexual Relations
of Production

The story turns next to a neglected but important dimension of women woods workers' lives with men in field work. We have seen that women confront a series of obstacles to full integration: difficulty gaining access to field jobs and supervisory experience; stereotyping in job placement and informal patterns in the division of labor; considerable testing of ability and attitude, especially women's physical limitations and their attitude toward male protection and assistance. Trying to become a "ladylike buddy" is a dominant model of accommodation many newcomers to field crews use to manage these and other difficulties.

A pervasive sexual undercurrent also underlies these shared working lives, as women enter territory as traditionally off limits to them as Paul Bunyan's living room could ever be. A portrait rich in sexual imagery emerges from these conversations, including three main themes: sexual innuendo in everyday routine; co-worker romance and affairs; and sexual harassment and abuse. These were issues raised by women field workers, the timber cruisers and beaver trappers and trail guards of the Forest Service. It is important to understand clearly that these aspects of a sexualized workplace are not unique to the Forest Service—far from it. In a great many organizations and occupations, the issues surface if only we ask the right questions. Nor do these themes dominate daily relations or typify interaction between women and men in the woods. The jokes and calendars, slurs, and embraces considered below are not characteristic of every department, nor even of most. But, as in the protection racket dynamic, while not all women nor all men are touched identically by this ambience, it nonetheless helps define the context in which women enter field crews. Breaking the silence about these topics helps us see another way male co-workers in the woods define the place of women asking to share their jobs and their company.[1]

Sexualizing the Workplace

The ubiquitous emphasis on the salience of sexual meanings in the presumably asexual domain of work takes many forms and is expressed differently under different conditions. It encompasses the relative use of "off-color" language and jokes, the tendency to "sexy talk," "girlie calendars" and "men's magazines," the interest of men in women co-workers as potential sexual partners (however improbably), and emphasis on women's appearance, marital status, and sexual lives. The resulting atmosphere lends to each work site a particular tone and impinges on the mutual definitions of workers and the workplace. For some women such sexualization is all too apparent and asks too much; for others, it is precisely what makes their work lives meaningful and friendships at work so special.

Language and Humor

In woods work as in other outdoor, working-class jobs the freedom to swear—elaborately and unabashedly—seems taken for granted. Even the most conservative workers share to some extent in this common argot: "It's the woods work that does it to you." After a brief period of uncertainty when newcomers are tested in this regard, patterns are established and tolerances defined. Many times women are initially presumed to dislike "raunchy" language for everyday use, particularly by those older men (especially in the office) for whom obscenity and femininity are incompatible. Others initiate a fairly intense period of testing—"grossing out" the new woman, if possible. Very often they are surprised when the newcomers join freely in swearing, sometimes even successfully turning the tables and "outgrossing" the competition. Occasionally this is a matter of deliberate strategy. This woman "had the experts give [me] lessons," and it paid off: "It didn't phase me, and for every remark fired in my direction, within a matter of seconds one was coming back. They knew it was going to be back, and we'd get into a contest, to see who was going to get who embarrassed first! And most of the time I had no problem . . . , because I was catching them so off guard to be talking that way in the first place and to be sounding like a man."

Not all men share this routine obscenity any more than do all women field workers; religion or upbringing, age and generation all create different levels of tolerance. Some see it as a matter of social class. To the upper-middle-class urban woman, adoption of routine swearing was a matter of strategy, the most effective means to "communicate with these people," though like many others she carefully monitors her language at home with family or friends.

Women often take a certain pride in their competence in obscenity. "I'll bet you a nickel there is nobody more wanton than a crew of women," one old-timer asserts. The eventual easy sharing in the pleasures of obscenity becomes for many women an indication of acceptance. This woman's co-worker voices the sentiment echoed so often: "If you're going to be doing this job with us, you're going to *be* one of us." She describes the typical development over time: "Probably the first couple of weeks of the '77 summer, right before I was trained, I didn't say too much, just the regular hells and damns, but the guys—I never heard 'aw fuck,' that one I didn't hear for awhile. And then after they all loosened up and we went to that training together, and everybody was a good guy, we were all in it together, one for all, all for one stuff—I heard everything."

There are limits, however. Distinctions are made by both sexes between routine obscenity and "really raunchy" talk that embarrasses some women. Except for those men seen as "show-offy" or determined to shock, this more extreme language seems to be limited when women and men work together. Women's freedom to swear is also constrained by implicit understandings that it not go too far. One man in the office complained to the supervisor about a young woman's casual and frequent use of "fuck," for instance, though for women to complain even informally about men's language most often meant more, and not less, abusive language.

While obscenity is rooted in sexual terminology, it rarely maintains any hint of the sexual when routinely used as the preferred language of the younger generation of workers. Participation in sexually tinged jokes, formally or casually related, can be a kind of badge of acceptance too. Dirty jokes, from "just normal everyday dirty joke time" to those jokes "below the gutter," are also characteristic of this setting. When the men they work with no longer feel constrained by their presence, many women feel a genuine sense of solidarity: "He said it's more fun now that he's getting to know me. When he first went out with me into the woods he felt kind of uncomfortable, that he couldn't be himself, that he was supposed to be this gentleman and everything. But now he feels like he can be himself and jokes around, says dirty little comments and things like that to me! I joke back with him and everything."

Successful presentation and acceptance of jokes, the telling and listening and laughing, can express status hierarchies within groups.[2] Thus women's participation in this activity establishes a claim to membership and sophistication, demonstrates tolerance, and distinguishes them from other, less "easygoing" women. And many do share in the jokes, though they must sometimes insist on their right to join: "They'll start telling a joke, and they'll say 'Shut your ears!' And I'll give them some kind of lip about it—'If you don't tell me I'll scream so loud that nobody else will hear it!'"

Less widely enjoyed, though also characteristic of many women field workers' situations, is casual discussion of male sexual activity, preference, or intentions—that is, "talking dirt." Not as prevalent as cussing while fighting heavy underbrush or fixing a flat tire, such talk has an altogether different flavor and sets a different tone. There are more objections to it than to swearing and jokes combined. Some women are surprised at their own naivete; one wondered, "Gee, do people talk like this all the time?" when she first heard her co-workers talk about a woman they knew. A solo woman in a crew of men reports being quizzed each Monday morning on whether she too "got laid" that weekend, and another has a male partner anxious to recount the "notches on his belt" as a married man.

These discussions occur in the pickup on the way to the unit, on the trail, or perhaps during a lunch break with contractors or loggers and may go on at length. In some crews male sexual activity forms the basis of most conversation and tests the tolerance of even the most patient women. Most do not share so freely in this talk, though it is usually difficult to avoid hearing and may be designed for effect. They wonder whether their very presence elicits this unsolicited suggestive commentary or whether this is normal male conversation. Although it may be staged for their benefit, often it is also simply routine: "The people I worked with—fucking women, drinking, and beating each other up was the only conversation *all day long*. . . . [No], these guys weren't into sports!"

Pin-ups, calendars, so-called men's magazines, and the occasional soft-porn paperback also express the sexualizing of the workplace. When the young men she worked with hung up such a calendar in their shared work space, one woman said nothing but wondered later: "They've always disturbed me, I don't know why. Maybe it's the mystique that's built up around them—they've got to keep them in the corners. I don't know, but it does bother me. . . . Maybe it's real hard for me when I'm working out in the woods to relate to something like this, because . . . 'I don't want you to look at *me* this way,' you know?"

Sometimes pictures and calendars were removed just before the first woman joined the department and shared the office or truck; she was then to blame for their loss, although the decision may not have been hers. Some women respond by hanging up *Playgirl* centerfolds; more often they simply threaten to do so but refrain from "starting *that* war." They may instead enjoy the discomfiture of some men when women openly discuss sex, birth control, or the bodies of favorite movie stars.

There are limits here too. Most sex magazines are kept in the men's bathrooms and are evident because of the snickers and jokes; sexy posters in offices visited by the public are rarely tolerated for long. Magazines and pictures which might offend are not often thrust upon women, though most are aware of the "smut drawer" maintained by certain men and the propensity of some to decorate their lockers with pin-ups. Most women feel quite able and willing to assert some degree of control; objectionable pictures, for instance, are unacceptable on the walls of a shared office, but it is "his privilege" to bring them to work if they are placed, like family pictures, under his own glass desk top. Again, some women take a certain pride in their tolerance of what to others is intolerably offensive material degrading to their sex. Overall few find it a real issue. Just as dirty jokes are something to take up time, the morning stop for coffee and the latest magazine to "read" on the drive to the work site may be "something we share" and laugh over as a group.

Innuendo, Modesty, and the Female Body

The infusion into the workplace of sexual themes of varying intensity takes other forms. Innuendo colors the most routine and normal activity to sexualize the asexual—from going to the bathroom or working alone with a woman to the size and covering of women field workers' breasts. Routinely, men and women are reported to be "just kidding" about sexual things in a friendly way. While rarely meant or taken seriously, such talk does enhance the sexual definition of women, and they are sensitive to it. Suggestive commentary abounds when a man and a woman return from a day in the field together or when one woman works with a number of men—"how was it?" "six at once?" When a crew of twenty men has one woman, a "harem" is pronounced. When exercises for agility places all members of a group flat on their backs with legs outstretched, the woman present is kidded: "nice spread—do you do that all the time?" And when walking into the brush to pee, male bosses crack jokes, inviting the woman to "lend a hand" if she'd like.

Female sexual naivete is tested as sexual connotations are attached to the most innocent remarks and each double entendre fully elaborated. Only rarely are women genuinely shocked, though a number consciously "play dumb" to change the subject and get on with the job. Such humor occurs inside offices and in the presence of upper-level career workers as well as on the more familiar crew level in the field. More than one woman has been embarrassed by the jokes (or the magazines, or the language) when in the presence of high-status managers—their district ranger, for instance. When powerful men might observe it, the implications are suddenly clear.

In the course of their work the same men and women may share a tent on an unexpected overnight in the woods without sexual overtones of any kind, may strip down for a welcome dip in a stream after an especially hot day in the woods, and generally manage to maintain friendly but nonsexual relations during their time together. In other ways their working lives are sexualized at every turn. Sexual overtones color even such facts of life as urination.

Considerable attention initially went to the question of where field-going women would pee in the woods in the absence of formal "comfort stations," and the issue remains alive for some. The objection is common when women enter other nontraditional places and jobs, though it is rarely an insurmountable problem—and never less so than in the lush Oregon forests. Nonetheless, the prospect of women bereft of private bathrooms is horrifying to some, men and women alike, though not to women who routinely work in the woods. Some men report a certain anxiety at first, wondering about the impact of women co-workers on the casual habit common in all-male crews of simply turning their backs to each other when necessary. Occasionally a story surfaces of a woman (usually very young) who is embarrassed to acknowledge her need and carefully limits liquid intake during the day.

Some women complain of not being able to share the advantages of male anatomy, while others are content to enjoy the break in work provided by a foray into the brush. Only a few circumstances make this a problem; for example, when working the fire line surrounded by men in a smoldering and denuded landscape, or when the privacy of the woods is some way off and the walk puts her behind the pace of those others who simply "check the tires" instead. Many women have stories to tell of embarrassing—now humorous—incidents involving unexpected encounters with men at inauspicious moments.

For most men and women, the bathroom quandary is no quandary at all. This unavoidable part of the working day is treated as the simple matter it is: women generally seek cover of some kind, and men generally at least turn their back to co-workers, though they vary widely in how far away they walk first. Modesty is a personal matter, and some men walk farther for privacy than some women.

Even in this context, however, a sexually suggestive atmosphere sometimes develops. Women who "drop their pants" as freely as their male counterparts quickly earn a reputation as "loose" women. The snickers and giggles which sometimes attend women field workers' search for protective covering lend an unwelcome tone to what is unavoidable. Though they are rare, a few men (often well known) worry women. They may follow a woman into the brush or arrange to be near her; others seem to draw attention to themselves deliberately by wisecracks or by not turning their backs to the women near them while peeing. Standards of normal, relaxed social intercourse which comes so easily in other parts of life suddenly take on new meaning here in the woods, even in so manifestly asexual a context as this.

A similarly suggestive atmosphere surrounds the working woman's appearance, particularly the degree to which she allows her female form to be evident. As in other male-dominated jobs, women on new turf face the familiar complaint that they are too disturbing for men to work around, at least when their sex is clear. For some the answer is to deemphasize in any way possible such clues to gender as hairstyle, form-fitting clothes, or jewelry. Like the others, they wear jeans and heavy shirts, layered clothes, long underwear, and heavy boots. Anything which draws attention to a woman's sex is avoided, and the field outfit itself becomes a kind of protective coloration, a camouflage of sorts to facilitate her integration.

When summer temperatures soar and many men work shirtless whenever possible, women occasionally wear halter tops, light T-shirts, or bikini tops. The charge of distraction surfaces then or when the absence of a bra is undisguised by layered clothing. To avoid the ribbing and ogling to which they have seen other women subjected, many make bras a part of the uniform and never relax their self-imposed dress code. More women would like the freedom of movement afforded by working braless, though still only a minority indulge the inclination, and fewer still without taking pains to hide the fact. The brave woman who removed her shirt altogether when her male partner did never again had to envy his coolness—"it blew him away." This is precisely the kind of pointed behavior to which many men object. The notorious women of contract tree-planting crews may work braless or shirtless when appropriate, but such freedom is slow in coming to the Forest Service.

While men joke about braless women "making me a little happier while I work," the more pronounced feeling is that women who do not disguise their sex in essence "flaunt—or taunt it" and that this display is somehow unfair to men. One young man strongly objects when his co-worker wears shorts, complaining at being "forced to work under those conditions," though he is otherwise an active participant in the sexual bantering so characteristic of the workplace. After being explicitly told how disturbing she was to the crew without a bra (and feeling terribly guilty about it), one woman was outraged when the same distracted men one day calmly stripped down for a quick swim, apparently thinking nothing of it.

Neither nudity nor revealing clothes are inherently sexy, of course. Heterosexual tension is no more inevitable when mixed groups skinny-dip than is homosexual tension when all-male groups swim nude together. Yet women's bodies are made sexual and their presence at work made distracting. The more clearly a woman is female, the more her presence seemingly distracts and the more tenuous her claim to legitimacy as a worker.

This sexualizing of the workplace also touches on family life. Stories are told and retold and are sometimes distorted (or perhaps intentionally elaborated) by the time they reach lovers and spouses at home. One woman tells of overhearing a man on her crew telling his wife that she raced through the forest in bikini underwear, totally misrepresenting the reality of her panicked flight from a hornets' nest. Many women know precisely how the men at home would feel about the sexual coloring of the language and humor and interaction at work, and they try to keep work and home quite separate, much as they refrain from mentioning what they actually do at work (e.g., when they use power saws or work alone). The sexual undercurrent is especially meaningful when real intimacy develops over time between co-workers, when all goes well. One woman's voice registered dismay when she told of the day her husband, also a Forest Service worker, worked with her on detail—"my crew *and* my husband" she said, as if the contradiction were clear, as if all members of the crew were her lovers. Another husband in a Forest Service couple was said to be upset by the talk and the jokes only when his wife was around; working separately, neither was disturbed. Some men take great interest in women's appearance, as well as in their marital status, likely attitude toward sex, tolerance for flirtation and physical contact, and sensitivity to innuendo.[3] Many women find this interest entirely normal, for "men will be men," or as one man put it, "if it's there, I'm going to look." New women joining the district or crew are routinely checked physically and are rated by some on the proverbial one-to-ten scale. Being eternally evaluated by any or all men can be painful. One woman recalls vividly the day she overheard the running commentary of men in the office on the body, walk, hair, and general appearance of a friend of hers who was walking by the window outside. It dawned on her that they must talk of her in the same way. She later whispered her hatred—of their incessant "jokes," their barely concealed disappointment in her weight gain, the need always to disguise her resentment, in fact (and here she was barely audible) her emerging hatred of men. She had come thousands of miles to her job and liked it, but now wondered how long she could stand it. Worst of all is the dishonesty: "Nobody knows how much I really hate it, nobody."

Like many women, she joins in the casual flirtatiousness characteristic of so many offices, drives, and lunch breaks. This flirtation usually expresses companionship and familiarity rather than sexual tension. One young woman ruefully remarked that on her summer crew there was so much kidding around that it was virtually impossible for anyone to initiate a serious sexual relationship. A kind of immunity to this tension is sometimes attained on the basis of marital status or male attachment, age or appearance; mothers and grandmothers, however, are sometimes equally active participants. Women otherwise protective of their privacy occasionally advertise a boyfriend or lover in order to defuse the situation. As a "taken woman" they escape some of the pressure. Then, too, when the boundaries are clear, flirtation is more relaxed and playful. This flirtatiousness is distinct from the hustle and come-on with which so many women must learn to deal. While it contributes to the context of romance and affairs, it is quite different, often expressing nonsexual affection and familiarity. There are other ways in which men and women can and do relate, and it is striking to see sexual overtones so consistently giving life to these new friendships.

Inclination to join in the sexual innuendo of the workplace is differentially distributed. While all women must respond to it, it is not confronted in equal intensity everywhere or by all female workers or at all times. The familiar distinction between professional and nonprofessional classes of workers surfaces. Indulgence in this aspect of workplace culture is often attributed to the "less educated" men on the crew level rather than to the "church-going family father." Similarly, the prevalence of sexual magazines and pictures in the fire and engineering departments is seen as a natural consequence of the generally lower status of workers there.

While sexual undercurrents are more overt in some places (and fire is the outstanding example), the atmosphere touches every part of the organization. In the higher-status fields of timber or recreation, there is simply more pressure for a self-consciously professional demeanor. It is partly a matter of professional socialization, and the "professional woman" serious about her career must watch her language as much as does her male professional counterpart. Also, while pin-ups can be tolerated in the warehouse, the district and zone offices in which permanent professionals work are generally open to the public, and the protection of the image of the Forest Service is taken quite seriously. Many observers emphasize that by comparison with the other men in the woods (chiefly the loggers), Forest Service men are considerably restrained; they are, after all, public servants.

These distinctions are secondary to the general sexualization of everyday working life, and they are also in transition. Increasingly women talk like men, and the new breed of professionals sounds like the organizational underclass. As one professional woman remarks: "I sometimes think it's crossed lines. . . . It's hard to tell who's what anymore."

Job characteristics structure the expression of these themes in the sexualized workplace. For instance, sexual bantering and casual flirtation are much more likely during slack periods and are thus prevalent in field jobs involving long drives or periodic office work. More independent workers share in the flirtation less because their time together is more limited. Some districts are dominated by managers with conservative styles which set the tone for acceptable banter. The opportunity for bralessness to arise as an issue is naturally influenced by ideas regarding the clothes that are appropriate for each job; for example, in fire fighting, correct clothes are critical for safety, and comfort takes second place. Those who work in remote areas far from the unexpected supervisor or "green fleet" enjoy more opportunity for a quick dip in a lake or stream.

Management style in each department and district influences the degree to which rules are enforced, including those concerning swimming, shirtless garb, mandatory hard hats, and so forth. Women report that the most insistent innuendo comes from those men not already used to working with women. Male newcomers on integrated crews apparently find the mode of relationship simple and compelling. Younger men direct their attention more toward those in their age group than to co-workers known to be grandmothers. In these and other ways, the sexualizing of women field workers and work relations varies in frequency and intensity, though it touches the lives of all.

Tolerance and Challenge

One of the principal challenges to women field workers is to respond acceptably to the sexualization of the working culture they enter. Women's attitudes vary dramatically on each of the themes raised here, from language use to flirtation. These differences reflect organizational and social class, feminist consciousness, and generation and life-style more than any kind of philosophical or religious conviction. With few exceptions, these women are not prudish—far from it.

Nonetheless, they hold two fairly distinct views. Many feel that the language, magazines, jokes, and general atmosphere created are all in a day's work and differ little from those they encounter in dealing with brothers, husbands, or friends. Others can hardly contain the resentment they feel, especially their inability to object effectively without demonstrating the anticipated reaction. Regardless of their attitudes, most women are prepared, and nearly all are resigned: "I know that's what they *do*. Living with [him] I know that—I know the Forest Service boys pretty well."

As newcomers women are particularly vulnerable to the charge of demanding change and special conditions, in this case imposing arbitrary and unfair restrictions on natural male pleasures. With few exceptions, however, most women seem to go out of their way to be accommodating. It is not they who remove pin-ups or insist that language or humor be "toned down" in their presence. Indeed, they are often the first to acknowledge these privileges of their male predecessors. One woman may define *Hustler* as pornographic, but more agree with the woman who equates her partner's right to have it in the truck with her right to study for night school exams on the way to work when it is his turn to drive. Women often sense a test, one they very much want to pass: "Oh, sometimes . . . it'd just be like dirty jokes, and I'd get embarrassed, and they'd laugh at me. But it was all in fun. They were just giving me a hard time. A lot of it I think was to make me feel more at ease and to get me in . . . kind of into their circle, because I wasn't. And after a while, quite a while, I started kidding them back, and it became a two-way thing."

The issue is often posed in terms of tolerance—theirs, for the men who were there first. As minority members of the crew, as newcomers, often as the only woman in a passel of men, many feel strongly that they have no legitimate claim on the kind of atmosphere they work in:

No, to me it would be wrong to try to change it. Because, you know, that's been their world for all those years, and I think you'd be really asking for troubles if you stepped in and said, "Here I am, now change!" Well, I felt like I *asked* to become part of that. In other words, I could have stayed in an office, or I could take a job where I would be protected from some of those things. I certainly wouldn't want men stepping into *my* world, you know. I resent *that*.

Women who object—who do battle to remove offensive calendars or who discourage flirtation or decry sexual innuendo—raise fundamental questions of privilege and deference and face the consequences. More often than not objections backfire; not only does the behavior or atmosphere persist, but it may well intensify, and those women who object develop reputations as "women's libby," inflexible, or puritanical. They do not "know how to take it" and raise the specter of "special privileges," though they would work in a man's world. One little story appears repeatedly in different guises, though the ending is the same. The speaker worked for a month at an indoor job with "three of the grossest people you'll ever meet." She continues: "Luckily, they abandoned ship and left me alone to do all their work! But you know, I was really kind of happy afterwards. They were just really gross. Everything was sex, sex, sex. I don't know if they were trying to embarrass me or make me feel . . . uncomfortable or just make me say 'Oh, I can't stand this anymore! Why don't you guys shut up!'" Later she was asked by another man how things had gone between them, and when she confided that she had found them "really gross," he began the familiar refrain: "'Well, *yup!* Something you're going to have to get used to. You're going to work in a man's world, you're going to . . . !' And I just thought, 'Oh my God, why did I ever say it?!'"

In the final analysis women's feelings are essentially irrelevant. The terms of their admission, the conditions under which they are accepted as co-workers in the woods, are set and enforced by men. Though some welcome any impact women can have in toning down the "hard-core" atmosphere at work, others insist upon tolerance and define acceptable "qualified" women as the "good sport" who goes along. But a woman's language, humor, and ways cannot go too far; as we have seen, the working buddy must be a "lady" too. Women's conditional participation in the sexualizing of work relations reinforces the critical sense of difference and deference underscoring sex segregation.[4]

Romance and Affairs at Work

Organizational expressions of interpersonal attraction are important to consider, for the job consequences for women field workers are profound. Organizational analysis and studies of women's work rarely touch this aspect of the informal organization, although as more women enter traditional male domains, we can expect more prevalent sexual or quasi-sexual work relations.[5]

Work is one of the principal places people meet and spend time together and sometimes (regardless of intention or commitment) fall in love and make love, becoming close friends or sometimes simply lovers. This is not the same point as that made so often by Dear Abby's correspondents and feared by many of the old guard in the Forest Service— that is, that simply because women and men work together, sexual liaisons are inevitable. In our society, as in others, there is a deep-rooted fear that real wives are threatened by "office wives," that the woman who "got there on her back" is probably still at it, and that the women after "men's jobs" are also after men. All these concerns are raised in earnest as women enter an occasional male preserve, in this case joining men on the trails, in the rigs, and at the fire camps.

What makes the private affairs important (whether sexual, only apparently so, or only sometimes so) and different from those initiated at parties or bus stops is the generally greater economic vulnerability of the female partners in on-the-job romances and their lower and more tenuous organizational status (leaving aside for the moment the question of relative emotional investment). They simply have more to lose, and in the Forest Service, as elsewhere, they do often lose.[6]

Jealousy and Rumor

Sexual relationships with men at work can end badly for women, culminating in jobs left, contacts lost, friends alienated, and bad transfers. Equally devastating and far more common are rumor and innuendo affecting women's reputations. Professional and personal reputations are always jumbled, but for women the sexual component is pronounced, travels fastest and farthest, and lingers.

Responsibility for sexual relationships is generally attributed to women, and it is their reputation which suffers. Women reputed to be "loose" may be enjoyed in some respects, but they are not groomed as future district rangers. Referring to his experience on seasonal brush disposal crews, this man sums up his impressions of the prospects of women with different styles and reputations: "All in all, my overall impression, the ones that were more easily accepted were the ones that the men could kind of say 'heh, heh, heh'—snicker about. 'Look at *that* one. I wonder what *she* does. . . . ' [The woman who] wears a low-cut top, and kind of plays around and flirts and teases with the men, goes ahead—at least as far as they'll put her."

While women's reputation as sexually active may sometimes facilitate acceptance on the crew level, there are also immediate and long-term negative consequences. One woman's determination to avoid sexual relations at work was strengthened by what she saw around her:

> You know, there's some women out there that do date . . . , and that's fine for them. . . . But I guess that's my little personal philosophy. . . . But I also know, when a woman has been going out with one of them and they break up, and she goes out with another one, there's a lot of talk, about *her*. And she's also the woman, instead of the worker. And I know that harms a lot of those women in their careers.

The lingering definition as "woman instead of worker" affects professional and nonprofessional women alike but is probably more destructive for professional women embarking on Forest Service careers, for obvious sexual activity or relationships are eminently unprofessional and less likely to be tolerated at this level. Women usually know this fact, but knowing does not always solve the problem: "I had a situation where, through working with a man and mutually really respecting the shit out of each other, just through that *bond,* it went to a sexual thing, because I was stupid and didn't know where to stop it. It was a very messy thing. . . . Now that I'm here, they've got this renewed interest in me *there.* Any woman that works over there knows about my trip." She complains later of her persistent identification as a woman open to sexual involvement with co-workers, noting that each time people from different districts meet (perhaps at training sessions or fires), the stares and comments are renewed—"Oh, you devil you!" She is not alone in wishing she could undo her past, though at the time it was mutually compelling and satisfying.

Women planning careers in the Forest Service must be especially attuned to this aspect of their reputation, as the system rewards those who transfer widely and wisely. Women are extremely visible everywhere, and those who move up in professional or technical positions are even more so. Old schoolmates, casual friends, former lovers, and former district rangers may all be met again some day, in another district, national forest, or region.

Reputations, as fleeting and imprecise as they are influential, are constructed largely of rumor and innuendo. Rumors with sexual overtones circulate fastest and furthest. When particularly nasty ones circulated about the first woman ever to work in a powerful department, they were attributed to "the epitome of the macho man—you know, big truck, big rack, big dog" who "had to put her down somehow." Field-going women may be taken to bed for similar reasons or may find themselves objects of male sexual fantasy: "He was in awe—fascinated. He just couldn't leave me alone, from the moment I got there."

In some cases the level of gossip and intrigue is so high that women opt out of activities helpful to their careers, for example, participation in fire management teams or training sessions involving out-of-town travel. The cost in gossip may be too high to ask a husband or lover to bear, and the risks to a peaceable family life may be judged too great. Exposure to powerful people provided by these activities is invaluable for those who know and care about careers, as many women do. But sometimes the threat to a budding romance or a worrisome marriage is more important. As one woman put it, "They know what *they* do" (e.g., at project fires or off-forest meetings) and assume the worst of women too.

Districts and departments also develop reputations. Some husbands and lovers express real fears that the women in their lives will take jobs at certain districts or will work under certain men or in certain circumstances. Promotion to jobs requiring odd hours and extensive overtime or assignments as the solo woman on a male crew are examples of job decisions which are often controversial at the dinner table. Some work situations raise the issue more than others. The man whose sweetheart joined the crew he only recently left knows how often all strip down for a quick swim, and she complains of his incessant quizzing as to whether or not she joined in. Some men at fire camp seem to take a little "fireside romance" for granted when women come along, and the concerns of boyfriends and husbands must be allayed when a project fire is called in.

Most women proudly report they enjoy trusting relations with husbands or boyfriends who are not unduly jealous. But the prospect that emotional intimacy will develop within crews does keep some husbands awake at night, especially those familiar with the Forest Service, as many spouses and boyfriends are. The threat of intimacy with other men, sexual or not, motivated one man to ask his partner (in an "open marriage") to quit her job. In fact, this growing companionship and closeness can be extremely gratifying; though rare, it means a lot to women. To some it simply points out "how unclose I was to my own husband." To others it is enlightening: "It gives me a chance to know them *other* than in a sexual connotation. . . . And I think I probably like men better because of it, because I have gotten a chance to know them as people rather than just men."

Men and women in the field often become physically and emotionally close, and it is not always easy to keep relations nonsexual. The lover of the woman quoted below also works on mixed-sex field crews, and together the two are coming to grips with this new element in their long-standing relationship. She finds herself much in sympathy with the familiar stereotype of the jealous wife. As both of them know, sometimes this precious intimacy ever so gradually comes to mean more:

> The thing is, the big thing is, that the wives fear about—which is really a true fear—is that you are sharing a really important part of her husband's life with him. And you *do* get tight . . . , and because I know that really well whenever [he] works with a woman, I know exactly what's coming down, and I have to learn how to handle that too. I know exactly what's coming down—I know they're getting tight.

Because in her own experience this intimacy has eventually led to a sexual relationship, she joins other lovers and wives in a certain remoteness from other women who work with men. If only subtly, field-going women register a certain tension between themselves and the wives and lovers of the men at work, and some worry about it. "Vicious" wives reportedly make life miserable for some field-going women, and at least one has had to deal with threatening early morning telephone calls from a jealous wife. A number of tactics help defuse the situation, including drunken tête-à-têtes and deliberately arranged meetings. Some emphasize the importance of simply being seen—in all their individuality, with their own lovers, and with fat and wrinkles too. This recognition is not always enough, and sometimes tensions rise intolerably. In one remote district with a number of single women and unemployed wives only a formal meeting smoothed things over: "The women who were being berated or whatever called in all the wives for an evening meeting, chewed it all out. . . . And then they had the meeting of the husbands and wives . . . and it straightened it all out. Because the women have the one side—'my husband's running around with *you* all day.'"

Several factors condition the intensity of jealousy. More problems develop when single women work with married men, particularly in one-to-one situations. When the community is very small and isolated, or when the Forest Service is the community and workers live in government compounds, the situation is exacerbated. But rumor and jealousy are no more restricted to geographically remote areas than are sexual liaisons. Some workers report fewer problems of jealousy in fire, where wives are familiar with irregular working hours and are more confident about what actually is going on. The problem is most acute when women field workers are new, unattached, and unknown. When there is communication and familiarity between wives and women workers, the situation is rarely explosive.

Broken hearts and marriages do occasionally result from very real on-the-job affairs. But men may exaggerate the theme, presuming to speak for women; "the wives won't stand for it" is an easy rationale for excluding women and is very difficult to challenge successfully. The sexualized atmosphere at work also adds intensity to the jealousy and mistrust which complicate marriages and relationships between spouses and field-working women. One married woman recalls hearing rumors of her involvement with not one but six men simultaneously, and found herself in the curious position of actually having to refute the rumor by meeting individually with wives. Sometimes such tensions are very difficult to resolve. One young woman was asked directly by her crew boss's wife if their relationship was sexual. Her denials were convincing, but the rumors spread and lingered:

> And all of a sudden this is when these rumors got started that I went to bed with the foreman of the tanker crew in order to get on the tanker crew. . . . I've been to bed with every guy on the BD crew. . . . I wanted to get into the office, so now I was going to bed with [him]. Enough is enough! And all these other women are all going through the same thing. I have no idea how they handled the situation, or whether they ignored it or how they dealt with it. But all of them, at one point or another would come back to the bunkhouse after work at the end of the day in tears, out of frustration—"Why are they doing this to me? Why can't they accept me for a human being, instead of some kind of an object? *What* do I have to do?" And I'm looking at them—"Hey, don't ask me. I'm still fighting the same battle. I've been here for three seasons now and I *still* haven't gotten it through their heads. I still have a reputation."

Male co-workers agree that many men are "on the make" at work. They look forward to mixed-sex crews in order to "meet some ladies" and are generally inclined to see a woman sexually first. While some are sensitive to the contradiction between relating to women as job partners and as "potential bed partners," others confidently assert that there is no problem in distinguishing women's "stature as a worker" from women's identity as "sex object." This sexual attention is often subtle and playful, but not always. Women complain that managers play "matchmaker" with their job assignments and that for some grown men the only apparent way of relating to women is as "a whore or a dyke."

Setting the tone and limits of this attention is yet another of the woman field worker's responsibilities. Subtlety and tact are essential, though they may be difficult to muster with crew members who are "not into an after-work situation—'right here on the job, let's go!'" Not all are adept at fielding this sexual attention. The "come-on" at a bar is a familiar situation, but at work more is at stake. One woman's analysis illustrates the common conviction that the responsibility is ultimately hers:

I think this is one point that . . . needs to be subtle on the part of the woman that's doing it. I think that if you're obnoxious about it, they're going to be upset, because that seems to be a man's right, to cuddle a woman. And if you just completely turn them off of it, they're going to be upset. But if you kind of just let them know that you're really not interested, then they'll take it a lot easier. Which is maybe a lot of hassle, but it sure saves a lot of [trouble].

Another woman puts a finer point on the same feeling, alluding to the importance of the interdependence created by the job situation: "You try to be polite and nice. You don't want to hurt their feelings. You *certainly* don't want to make them mad, because you might need one of them some day to pull you out of a sticky situation, and you don't want *that* to get in the way." It may be, as an experienced woman argues, that unresolved sexual tension accounts for at least part of the evident hostility of some men:

The thing that happens is . . . most of the time they're not attracted. Most of the time what happens is somebody likes somebody, a man likes a woman, and there's this sexual tension. I've had male friends, and even if they're friends, there's always this tension. And they're very disappointed when you have a steady boyfriend. They're hurt. Whether there's a chance of you having a relationship with them or not, they're hurt. . . . Yeah, that option is closed. And that sexual tension, when not dealt with a good way, has developed into violence in the field. We've had supervisors who have just left women in the field, just left them out in the woods to stay the night.

Another woman seconds her opinion, noting how quickly her "buddies" on the crew grew distant when they learned of her serious relationship with a man unknown to them. More often, however, this reputation as "taken" by marriage or commitment is useful in eventually achieving a new and gratifying friendship with men.

The interdependence of work and the importance of smooth working relations ultimately persuade most women to do their utmost to keep serious relations at work nonsexual. Still, as one perceptive young woman puts it, "Sometimes there's something kind of basically sexual about a relationship . . . and you maybe get along together better because of that." The "sexual energy" motivating sexual relationships comes from both directions and is sometimes impossible to ignore or avoid. Women and men generally have little experience relating as co-worker, peer, or equal in circumstances uncomplicated by sexual tension. Some men attribute the difficulty to men's inexperience at "fraternizing" with women or at transcending the "courtship" mode which follows so naturally into the workplace. One thoughtful young man worries that real integration and sexual equality may involve doing away with courtship and marriage altogether, to broaden the ways in which the sexes interact comfortably. Sexual tension at work makes genuinely nonsexual friendships more valuable, especially to women and particularly in an atmosphere so pervasively sexualized.

The Management of Affairs

Sexual attraction does occasionally culminate in some degree of public relationship—from the scandalous liaison of the unit manager in the "Peyton Place twice over" district to fairly private affairs or fleeting on-the-job dalliance. Affairs at the field crew level, on which this book focuses, must be carefully managed organizationally.

The intensity of the isolated field crew means that workers quickly develop close relations—occasionally openly hostile, they are also occasionally romantic. The seasonal labor force in particular brings together many young and unattached people. Working in isolated areas, with long overtime hours and odd shifts, or living in crowded government bunkhouses in districts that provide them, creates the proximity and intimacy conducive to romance. Most affairs described involve single persons, both of whom are field going and temporary; most also involve men of higher status than their lovers. Full-blown affairs among field workers tend to be exogamous to the crew, though this is a fine line to draw, as crews are unstable groups shifting in membership, activity, and atmosphere between and during seasons. Many involve partners detailed temporarily to the crew or department or peers on different crews working closely together.

The need for relaxed and comfortable relationships at the crew level, so long together in isolated settings and so interdependent, makes anything impinging on the status quo important, much less something so dramatic as an affair involving crew members. There seems to be a lower tolerance for such affairs when the need for more cohesive crews is greater, though this tendency is modified by such factors as the discretion exercised between the lovers at work, the intensity of the relationship, and the status and power of the personalities involved. Criticism falls most freely on couples whose behavior affects the work of the group and on those who make their work secondary to romance. Love making does occur on the job (as one manager put it, "Now they go behind a tree, where before it was the stock room"), for field work allows the flexibility necessary to combine romance and work. By and large, however, lovers are conscientious: "Here I cut [her] down for doing the very same thing I did, but at least we got our work done first! When it was work, it was all seriousness. We knew we worked good together, and we knew we could get it done. And we were *into* that aspect of our relationship—how well we worked together." Another woman seconds the point, recalling how she insisted to her supervisor-turned-lover, "If this hurts our working relationship, I'll kill you!"

The organizational consequences of on-the-job romances are diverse. Chief among them is increased gossip, for even the most determined couples find their private relationships more or less public knowledge. One unlucky woman lived in a small apartment in a small town situated on the main route to the office. The visibility of the house and of the cars parked in front meant that all who passed could monitor the progress of a budding relationship. When the relationship ended, the two were forced to work together on the crew each day, and the young woman's pain was visible too:

> But it also affected her standing in fire control . . . because she was so moody. She'd get real short-tempered. . . . It meant that she couldn't work with a lot of people. It meant she was hard to get along with at work, during that span of time, which was about three months. . . . I think it just kind of ruined a lot of—not all but some of—her standing, I mean with people that during the next summer could have helped her out more.

Formal communication channels may be short-circuited by romance, as lovers move in and out of circles of information and gossip, bringing new insight and perspective to their job. Supervisors involved in romantic associations may be distracted or only selectively interested. Conversely, supervision can intensify when affairs at work mean that lovers happily put in long hours or pay sudden attention to tasks providing an occasion to meet. A bystander complains: "She would stick around with him waiting for him to go home so she was constantly in *my* way, constantly correcting me, and I couldn't carry on the job and do things the way I wanted to, like anyone normal would want to do." Affairs also result in the loss of key personnel sometimes, when transfers voluntary and involuntary separate or unite lovers. Broken hearts and lovelorn romanticism reshuffle people as much as career decisions or divorce, marriage, and remarriage.

These special relationships influence how daily work is accomplished, by whom, and how well. One excellent partnership was destroyed because the man disapproved so strongly of his partner's affair with a man on the crew. Other partnerships are created by the attraction itself. Crew bosses and supervisors sometimes purposefully separate lovers at work, as they do spouses. They feel that in time of danger, as during a fire, objective and cool-headed action may be difficult for lovers.

In some cases male lovers can help the women they care for, providing introductions, inside knowledge of job openings, formal and informal recommendations, or career advice.[7] In one case too an administrative woman was able to use her lover's influence to help get a number of women the field jobs they wanted, lobbying informally on their behalf. During a particularly tense time at a fire when she needed help, one woman recounted the special attention she got from a friend of her lover who remembered to look for her.

Affairs, rumors, and jealousies are all managed by the "family" at work as by the one at home, and sometimes they are mismanaged. One woman was forced to file a formal grievance against her supervisor to protect her field job; her lover's wife had demanded of the ranger that she be taken off the crew, and he had complied. In another case, a disapproving fire management officer marked one young seasonal woman's file "no rehire" because of her affair with the fire crew boss, and she was forced to move to another area to find work.

The public relations consciousness of the organization leads it to avoid scandal of any kind. Many in the Forest Service are convinced that management will not tolerate public affairs but will manipulate them through strongly suggested transfers or "talkings to." Government housing can also become a tool in the management of affairs, when unmarried cohabiting couples are threatened with eviction.

Unit management is only slowly moving away from the traditional model of the patriarchal family, and the manager or zone engineer is still very important in setting the tone as much as in laying down the law. Officially, members of the same family should not work under each other's direct supervision, nor should one work in a position of possible undue influence (i.e., personnel). In fact, there is wide variation in the interpretation and enforcement of this general policy. Under some managers husband and wife work in close association, even within the same department, while only a short distance away another couple may deliberately postpone their marriage in order to protect their respective jobs. In labor-short communities, wives are often welcomed into the clerical ranks, though the practice may otherwise be not to employ couples. While there has recently been more pressure to help locate jobs for spouses (something more and more Forest Service couples require), the traditional preference for hiring people who are unrelated often persists. In any case, most managers still happily ignore the tricky subject of what to do about unmarried yet enduring couples.

Sexual attraction rejected or reciprocated inevitably colors working relations. Women fending off passes from contractors, trying to manage civil relations with jealous wives, and watching bosses "put the move on" other women all testify to the influence of sexuality and the unity of social life. There can be no meaningful line drawn between on-the-job and off-the-job interaction of co-workers, nor between professional and personal reputations. The example below is a particularly harsh illustration of the general point: "My boss, when I first came here, was chasing every woman around here—oh man, it was disgusting! But as soon as we were at work, he was Mr. Nice. . . . And all of a sudden I'm supposed to buy this 'respect' act, when I'd seen him at a party two nights before making a fool of himself, throwing himself at everybody."

Perhaps the greatest significance of romance and affairs at work is the contribution each affair makes to sexualizing the workplace and suggesting the range of possible co-worker relations. Each woman's decision about dating men at work profoundly influences the reception of the next woman hired on to the crew or into the office. The graphic example below is not unrepresentative of the situation of many field-working women:

> The first day I got there I got shoved in the truck and taken to every single unit that the reforestation people were tree planting. "This is her! This is the new girl!" And I've never seen them do that to any other employee—and people coming up from the bottom unit to meet you, which you never do unless you have to! And then I got told that the girl who was there before me had "gone over the hill." [She laughs about not understanding and about hearing later about another woman who "had stated out loud that she was going to sleep with everybody in the district."] I guess she did a pretty good job, from what I hear. But things like that don't help. Because then they wonder.

Making the choice—to be "Polly Purebred" or to be open to romance and sex here, as elsewhere in life—is part of the larger question of how best to manage entry into a male domain. While the distinction is rarely so static or clear-cut (and "Mr. Right" may intervene) these different ways of managing sexuality at work are easy to trace and may account for some of the animosity which arises occasionally between women in the woods.

The difficulty comes in artificially separating romance and work, affection and friendship, and in parrying unwanted attentions and defusing sexual tension. This too is a challenge facing women as they learn to work in the woods with men, and it must be met in the context of a generally sexualized workplace culture. It is an issue never fully resolved and one source of the dynamic and contradictory relations between the sexes at work. It is enough to make some women wish they had never heard of the Forest Service.

Sexual Harassment

Occasionally, co-workers and bosses unable to accept women as occupational peers and colleagues express their resentment in overtly sexual fashion. Thus, in the Forest Service as elsewhere, one problem women workers face is sexual harassment.[8]

The term "sexual harassment" seems to mean too little and too much. When it refers to dirty jokes or pin-ups, for instance, it is better seen as part of the sexualizing of the workplace and work relations. On the other hand, it does not fully convey the reality of sexual violence against women workers or economic retaliation against those who reject powerful men and resist demands for sexual services. Sexual aggression and extortion can and should be singled out, and the term "sexual harassment" should be reserved for what it suggests—harassment, here called manhandling. It is interaction in and around the workplace which is sexually suggestive, objectionable, and nonreciprocal. Together, these different problems constitute a continuum of abuse, founded on women's fundamental economic and sexual vulnerability and reflecting a cultural tradition which sexualizes, objectifies, and diminishes women.

This study suggests how one organization has come to terms with the sexual harassment of women at work, and how its approach affects both daily work relations and long-range career prospects for women. In the Northwest the issue was sparked by one outstanding case and was taken up by women active in the Federal Women's Program. At both the regional and local level they met first with denial, then with ridicule, and finally with grudging acceptance of sexual harassment as a problem. It was as difficult for those who argued the case then as it is today for any woman who broaches the topic, although bureaucratic machinery has slowly been set into motion. Committees were appointed, conferences planned, women polled, and memos composed on this aspect of the dynamics emerging during sexual integration, just as organizational attention focused on racial tension as the labor force grew more diverse ethnically.

Administratively, sexual harassment is defined very broadly. A memo from the office of the regional chief administrative officer explains it as follows: "Sexual harassment, as defined by the courts, requires only these three elements: 1. An act or suggestion which is offensive to another; 2. A request that it cease; 3. Inaction or denial of the request to cease." Examples follow, ranging from "remarks or jokes about a person's clothing" to "overt threats regarding promotion possibilities," and women are advised that speaking up about what they do not like is "the most effective action to prevent or stop sexual harassment." The memo concludes: "In visiting with employees, I find that the area of sexual harassment is not understood. . . . This subject is complicated by the fact that there is no concrete definition of sexual harassment."

At the district level, one woman put it more bluntly:

> The issue was treated as a running joke by my male counterparts, the problem being—whose definition of sexual harassment is correct?! Unfortunately, all anyone could come up with were the negative aspects of any possible action that could be taken, i.e., false accusation, supersensitive female employees, . . . and mainly the old myth that "she was asking for it" by her dress, manner, movement, etc.

Paradoxically, because it came to the attention of upper-level personnel and is the subject of both official memos and informal discussions, the term "sexual harassment" has gained a certain notoriety and is not often used comfortably. The formal organizational definition is so broad it trivializes the concept and encourages only debate and confusion over its scope. Some confuse it with sex discrimination generally. For example, comments from men about women's physical ability represent sexual harassment because, as one manager puts it, they are "based on the difference between the two sexes." Others feel that the term should refer only to aggressive physical contact.

While the ambiguity bothers women, it bothers men more. The key issue is definitional. Many men wonder if sexual harassment is simply "in the eye of the beholder" and hence is intolerably idiosyncratic. And what distinguishes promotional posters of nude women selling chain saws from posters of Burt Reynolds? There is not yet a consensus even among women on boundaries between the acceptable and the unacceptable, and there may never be. Must men risk accusation of harassment as they learn each woman's personal feelings? How can managers judge the difference between a stare and a leer? These are the questions which spark intense argument, create bitterness and alienation, and intensify already tense relations between the sexes.

Women's discussions of sexual harassment during a women's program lunch meeting or over a beer provide an occasion for defining personal politics, boundaries, and modes of accommodation with male co-workers. The dominant paradigm, one shared by men, is that women are responsible for avoiding undesired suggestive interaction. Asked about her experience with manhandling, one woman voices the typical response:

> Oh yeah, we have one on the district that's great—not just me, but with everybody. But . . . he knows where he stands. . . . So like I say, I think it's how *you* react in those types of situations. I firmly believe that if that happens, it's as much the woman's fault—probably more so—because I feel you have to establish what you want, or what you are, as a person. . . . I can't think of any situations where I've ever had to worry about being . . . molested.

Not all field-working women are so certain, but as a group they are very sensitive to charges of false accusation. Does objecting to men who regularly massage your head when you meet mean in turn having to forgo the simple pleasures of flirtation? Is it necessary to "change my personality" to avert possible misunderstanding? How does a person intuit intent and meaning or interpret ambiguity in human interaction? The questions are complex and are posed in very subtle ways:

> Every once in a while I'll ask him a question and they'll come up to me, and it's not like they're just standing next to me, it's like—you know, they have to *lean* against you. And I just kind of move aside, and keep right on talking. But I've noticed it a few times. It's not like—I don't know, maybe it's a friendly gesture. It seems like sometimes you ask a question and you have all these guys that want to come in and answer your question. . . . I wouldn't do it to *them*.

Some things are clear: women have no trouble identifying unwanted and unsolicited physical intimacy, whatever term they may give it, when it happens to them. While disagreeing over tolerance to harassment, with about half the group pointing critical fingers at the women down the way, in their own stories, the blame falls clearly on men. One of the most vocal critics of women who complain of harassment objects to the man in the office who aims rubber bands at her crotch when she sits at her desk with legs loosely crossed. In her own case, she is sure his behavior and not hers is the problem.

A certain wariness between women and men is evident on these new grounds as they meet and mingle at work. Many men feel unfairly vulnerable to complaints of harassment, with far-reaching consequences for their carefully constructed personnel files. One professional man, for instance, suddenly became aloof from the woman to whom he had formerly paid much attention, for he heard through the grapevine that she was upset with him. He had pulled her down into his lap as she stood by his desk using his phone, and had given her a big kiss and a long bear hug when he caught her in a narrow hallway on her birthday. Because she was new and generally liked him she agonized about how to respond to his sudden coolness. She went to great lengths to arrange a private meeting to clear the air:

> I think he was more worried about—he *was* more worried that he was going to get reported and get into trouble. So I reassured him I wasn't the kind of person to do that. That was the main thing I was saying. We didn't really get into whether he could go ahead and do it. "I hope you're still friendly with me" is what I told him, that I didn't mind it *that* much, is what I told him. . . . I wouldn't ever have done that. I mean, I was ready to deal with it someday, in a better way. I wasn't going to go to some higher-up. But what I ended up doing is . . . , I was so worried about his being upset that I ended up trying to apologize to him, to tell him that it was really OK.

Women respond very differently to these gestures—from the casually placed hand (on breast or thigh) or uninvited bear hug, to bra snapping, pinching, or sudden kisses. The "roving hands" man is difficult to deal with, whether it is the new man on the crew who still persists in patting you when he passes or your supervisor who presses his thigh against your back while going over reports indoors. Each district or zone seems to have its "lech" around whom it is best to be cautious; his leering and touching eventually become part of the taken-for-granted world at work.

The tolerance of even the most tolerant women is sometimes tested, though in general the women seem remarkably patient—and with good reason, for theirs is a no-win situation. Not objecting to the casual fondle can be as devastating to reputation and status as labeling the caress sexual harassment. Avoidance is a strategy on which many women rely when possible; at other times embarrassment works, especially for women whose "fast mouth" can stop the roving hands publicly. Direct confrontation is less effective, as it generally leads directly to denial and charges of false accusation and misunderstanding. Physically direct responses, however, can do wonders. This case is the most graphic of the several like it. Polite objections to the "grab-ass feeler-type" man who made her and others uncomfortable seemed only to encourage him. The next time she did not stop to talk:

> I wasn't going to take it any longer. Enough is enough. He grabbed my ass, and I just came around and punched him right in the nose, and I said, "Goddamn it, keep your fucking hands off me. I don't want to be touched by you or anyone else!" Here's all these guys standing there—oh my goodness! I have a hot temper, but they had no idea that I would actually

physically get upset. . . . I never had any more physical contact with anyone unless it was supposed to be there, like in a situation where you had no choice, you were going to end up touching bodies because of what you were doing. . . . But even then, before that time, they could even make *that* make you uncomfortable. The *way* they would have their body rubbing against you, or the way they were working next to you, they were able to make you uncomfortable.

In other instances, direct action can be unwise. Surrounded by her all-male crew, one woman was thrown to the ground and repeatedly kicked by her crew boss, who screamed at her in rage, when their unpleasant verbal battles of the past weeks suddenly erupted in violence. She no longer lets herself be alone in the woods far from help when working only with men, and this stance is making it easy for her to be moved slowly out of the district altogether. No one will talk with her about what happened.

Acts of aggression need not be violent to be sexually abusive and frightening. One young woman on her first job found herself backed against the pickup door by one of the two men with whom she was out, as he openly began to masturbate while approaching her. The other man interceded eventually, and they rode back in silence. For weeks she kept the incident to herself. When she finally told her parents, they went directly to the district ranger. She quit her job and her co-worker was "talked to" about his "problem."

These incidents are, happily, very rare. The intimation of possible sexual aggression or violence is more significant than actual sexual abuse, which cannot often be repeated with effect or (one hopes) with impunity. These incidents become a part of the oral history of the workplace, create an atmosphere in which women count themselves lucky not to have been singled out, and generally take their place in the private troubles and fears of the night.

No easy generalizations emerge about sexual harassers. Women report problems with young seasonal workers skeptical of their place on the crew and with high-status professionals they see only rarely in the office. Harassers can be strange men at fire camps or very familiar local men. Some faces, in fact, are all too familiar. When persistent problems surface with an individual, management is tempted to "pass him on," from district to district, forest to forest.

The sexual composition of working groups is one source of variation in harassment and aggression, for the sex ratio of any group inevitably influences the group climate. Many women note that in everything from language or humor to physical intimacy, a viable one-to-one relationship quickly deteriorates when women are outnumbered. Most reported instances of harassment or aggression involved one man, often in a remote place, as do most cases of assault.

This aspect of working in "a man's world" is recognized by women, just as they were reared to be alert to the possibility of rape. For some there is always an element of fear in daily life at work, and they can never be fully prepared:

> You take a lot of trust when you get in a long rig that's sixty miles away with someone you don't even know. And it's like being attacked in your *home*. You feel very uncomfortable and unsafe in your own home. That's like scaring you in your safe zone, which is ten times more frightening than when you're working as a bartender and you *know* what the hell they're going to do to you—you're prepared for it, you're looking for stuff. But when they get you off guard, it's frightening, very frightening.

While Forest Service women do not live and work in fear, this recognition influences daily working lives in the woods. When the woman working in the fire lookout station high on the ridge is raped one summer, the woman taking that same station the next season enters the situation differently from the man or woman who held it the year before or who may work there next year. Women must avoid certain men—the one who raised a clenched fist to her when she was acting crew boss, or who followed her into the brush when she went to the bathroom, or those who never turn their backs to her when peeing. Word passes along the female network to newcomers warning against solo work with particular men, from the head of a department to a popular contractor or a noteworthy young "woods jock." Some women spurn this underground network of rumor and reputation as unfair, perhaps even paranoid, but it can help. One woman recalls the day she worked with a man accused by others of attempted rape; when he turned to relieve himself and then asked her pointedly if she would like to do so also, she knew better than to take that moment to walk off into the brush.

At fire camp the easy transition from fear of (some) men to protection by (some) men against others is especially apparent. Men otherwise hostile or indifferent often join in protecting female crew members ("our girls") from other, unknown men. It is a role in which many men and women take comfort. This woman's story suggests how fear facilitates male control:

> It was how they came on to me that made me uncomfortable. "*No*" didn't really make any difference. They were the type of guys that if you were to

haul off and smack them, they'd have smacked you right back, and then gone ahead and done what they were going to do in the first place. . . . So you were caught between this rock and a hard spot. . . . How do you get it through their head you're not into it, without making them mad? So I'd attempt just to avoid them as much as possible. . . . And a lot of the guys purposely made sure that the women didn't get stuck in a situation, working with them. . . . Although they came across dirty and nasty and what have you, you *don't* hit a woman, and you don't forcefully take anything.

Finally, the prospect of sexual blackmail threatens women's peace of mind at work. Attempted sexual extortion—using power over valued job characteristics, opportunities, or rewards to enforce sexual demands—is usually the prototypic instance of sexual harassment as most observers define it. There is no history of such blackmail in the field-going women's experience in these two study forests, at any rate not one overt enough to surface as a distinct issue. In contrast, the touching and leering, even the scaring—all are very much a part of the record in the short years women have come to work with men in and out of offices.

The data available, inevitably imprecise and incomplete, suggest the scope of sexual harassment and abuse in the Forest Service and their divisiveness as public issues in the workplace. Emotions and stories formerly underground now surface as legitimately part of the public debate over workplace conditions. In committee meetings and coffee rooms, sexual harassment is documented, interpreted, and debated. How is it managed organizationally?

Most managers now consider fielding complaints about sexual harassment part of their administrative responsibility. Directly or indirectly, sexual harassment and abuse impinge on management issues. For example, sometimes women cannot be assigned to inspect the work of particular contractors known for making insistent passes at Forest Service women. Work may be done quickly or carelessly to avoid someone, or authority may be undercut by fear. Workers are lost to the organization because they are "too sensitive" or because the price is too high. The atmosphere and mood of the entire district are profoundly shaped by the threat or reality of sexual harassment or aggression.

For some managers the question is much simpler, for sexual harassment is seen as a matter of human rights. No woman should have to confront a sexual harassing man, any more than she should be coerced into "riding with a crazy driver." Many managers feel that women on the district would come freely to them if need be. Others are not so sure but strive to create such a climate. The manager who argued that legitimating sexual harassment complaints only allows women to "decide here's something else [to] complain about" probably speaks for others too. He prefers not to give much attention to "an issue like that," which will only "make everybody start thinking about it . . . , and then you *will* get a problem."

Nonetheless, women can and do use bureaucratic channels to field complaints of sexual harassment, such as the equal employment opportunity counseling system at the district level. Complaints can be aired informally or concerned parties and their advisers can confront each other directly. Counselors also help facilitate the filing of formal complaints as a last resort. The system is geared to informal resolution of problems before they become full-fledged organizational dramas. Like most counseling, this form is predicated on the model of miscommunication and misunderstanding and relies heavily on talking things out. One skeptic accepts it as a bureaucratic "release valve" worth its weight in gold in defusing volatile situations and avoiding scandal.

While occasionally some action results (e.g., "her supervisor was reprimanded and sent to training sessions to improve his EEO and supervisory skills"), formal complaints are rare. Whether the machinery provides concrete help or simply cools out enraged women, it is rarely used. Male counselors may not provide the listening ear essential to a woman concerned about sexual harassment. And many women fear reprisal.

Activists committed to organizing women around the issue decry women's reluctance to make private complaints formal. Some are immobilized by fear of "blacklisting" and backlash, organizationally and personally. One frustrated activist adds: "As long as it isn't lethal, a lot of women don't want to—you know, as long as it's over with, they don't want the hassle." They are also often determined to demonstrate their tolerance as co-workers and to avoid scandal. As in rape cases, fear of reprisal coupled with the notoriety of the victim silences many women.

In the new and awkward climate created by public debate, most women scrupulously avoid self-definition as victims of sexual harassment. More often the debate—and it is a continuing process of definition and negotiation and boundary setting—takes place in the jokes and hints and gossip of the underlife of the organization, where most important questions are dealt with.

Summary

The workplace is sexualized when each opportunity for sexual innuendo is elaborated, from the magazines in the glove compartment to the natural shape and function of the body. The result is a working culture which sexualizes ostensibly asexual and routine dimensions of action and interaction. Though their participation is somewhat limited, many women find the culture familiar and satisfying, especially when it encourages flirtation and intimacy. Romance and sex also enter the workplace. Field workers and their families learn to deal with rumor and jealousy, and women in particular guard their reputations carefully. Affairs with co-workers can have disastrous personal consequences for women, though less negative results organizationally. Its impact on the organization makes romance a subject for management, and the issue is never fully resolved.

Finally, this chapter considered sexual harassment and abuse. Many factors discourage women from defining problems as sexual harassment, though they confront very real problems, including exhibitionism and physical intimidation. Harassment must be distinguished from sexual extortion and aggression; more common and routine, harassment is ultimately more important.

The heart of the matter remains the larger significance of hidden caresses, small jokes, and stolen kisses. These dimensions of the sexual relations of production reflect not the "natural" behavior of men but the context of segregation and integration, the assertion and challenge of the status quo. Sexualizing interaction with women newcomers helps neutralize or deflect the threat women seem to pose to the world in the woods that some men take such pleasure in. Introducing sexual themes at work is a mechanism of resistance uniquely available to men as they wage the battle of counterinsurgency against the presumptuous female intrusion.

6

The Limits
to Integration

One young temporary worker confessed to discouraging a friend intent on following her footsteps into forestry. "Don't do it! You're in for a world of pain and hurt." And she meant it. She wouldn't recommend it, but neither would she give it up. She is one of many women who persist, seeking ways of enjoying both their work and those they work with. They count themselves privileged to enjoy the pleasures of a day's work in the woods with a good crew. They feel respected as workers and valued as friends, and even the Oregon rain is warming. Yet time and again, the story begins with trouble, as field-going women talk of what worries and insults them, confuses and hurts. The roots of bitterness are tangled and can never be entirely clear. Still, though it may seem to come from everywhere at once without reason, there are patterns to male resistance.[1]

Women in the Forest Service working outside clerical roles are a constant irritant to some men, who in turn constantly irritate those women who must work near them. Territory difficult for some men is easy for others. Some object to the Federal Women's Program newsletter or to meetings for women only, while others worry only about the long-term impact of women on the reputation of the work group. Some take principled stands against working with women (or against work by women for wages), while others object only to inappropriate women in inappropriate places. Some opposition is rooted in recurring situations and is thus constantly regenerated, endemic to the workplace.

Conflict is likely when women and men must work closely together (e.g., in trainee positions, as temporary workers on summer crews, or as professionals sharing office and career path). Long drives to work sites, extensive overtime, or work in isolated settings all force interaction, providing an opportunity for aggravation missing in other jobs. Paradoxically, conflict is also common when relations are very distant. Between the female temporary technician and the permanent male professional there is room for a world of misunderstanding. Differences may be submerged by immediate concerns (e.g., safety, deadlines, or uncontrolled fire), and exaggerated by tasks demanding cooperation, as indicated below:

> I was just about ready to punch his lights out! Him I had a lot of trouble with. He's just another one of those who didn't think I knew anything. It's like, I'd been working on the crew for four months, and then he comes along and in two days acts like he knows everything and will *not* listen to anything I say. And, like, we have to work together. We were marking trees, which you really have to do together. You know, there are things you can get by without working together, but not marking trees.

Even alcohol has a role, for anger sometimes emerges only when emotions override manners. More than one woman has faced drunken insults from apparently friendly co-workers or supervisors. Hostility may be limited to certain realms of interaction ("he says he likes me—not between 8:00 and 5:00, though") and to certain places: "They thought it was pretty neat that I was on recreation, and I liked it an awful lot. I just loved walking through the woods. . . . But fire control was something just a little bit different. I guess it's just something that's really traditionally not women's work, with the muscles, the fire, the danger and everything."

A woman's relative skill is important, for as a neophyte she may be more easily accepted than women whose experience makes them crew bosses. The unskilled, young, cute, temporary worker is essentially "harmless," but the permanent professional woman aiming for a GS-7 has a harder line to walk. As women gain experience and skill and familiar faces are replaced by strange ones, the context of resistance alters. The professional woman reluctantly trained by a resentful male technician may move to a new job drawing on her strengths in a district with a history of good relations between the sexes. Her replacement, however, will face the old problems.

The sex ratio of the work group is influential, for isolated women are easier targets, and the antagonism of co-workers is strengthened when other men share it. The nastiest co-worker may not be around forever. Crew membership is fluid, and labor force mobility dissolves some intractable conflicts. The crew has a history, though, and each new woman is judged by her predecessor; if there was ill feeling in the recent past, trouble may loom ahead too. Women will face more problems on a crew of "animals" who pride themselves on ferociousness than on a trail crew with a history of amiability.

Field-going women learn to distinguish between versions of hostility. Implicit rationales are attributed by naming: the "short little shit" who fancies himself "God's gift to women" or those "into the 'I am a man'" routine differ from the occasional "bad apple" and yet again from the "organic earth mother" co-worker. The "new breed" or younger generation strike some women as infinitely more sympathetic to women in new roles. Others argue youthful "long hairs" are as likely to be the source of trouble as those "lifers" or "overhead types" who more often are blamed.

The real feelings of male workers may also be unclear or contradictory. Many women share nagging doubts about hidden judgments and secret reservations, wondering what friendly co-workers say about them in their absence. They complain also of familiar figures who "know what the official word is and know they have to be cool about it." Some suggest that false equanimity is more likely than unguarded hostility, as men grow leery of women's power of complaint and hence defensive. They also know of "macho but equitable" men and of those who espouse the "party line" but never have integrated crews or hire high-status women. One young woman recognizes the complexity of resistance and acceptance:

> I've talked to guys who talk as if they just see me in sexual terms, two in particular, and yet they have been really good about treating me just as an equal co-worker. Some guys talk as if—just saying what I want to hear—and then maybe they'll just give me all the light stuff to do, or in some way or another I'll feel they're treating me as if I'm not as capable, or being chauvinistic or whatever. Then there are other guys who will talk sort of sexistly and then they'll have me do just as much work or explain how to do something as if I was an intelligent human being.

Because stories circulate, most women have a sense of how things go elsewhere and often feel lucky by comparison. They attribute reasons to unreasonable behavior in an effort to discover how to prevent or parry hostility. Why was one woman the butt of constant suggestive commentary, while another seemed immune? Why must one fight constantly for the chance to do her own work, while others have trouble getting help even when they need it? After a long day of jokes (e.g., "maybe we could make her my driver—that's women's work") in which even her district ranger joined, one woman had finally had enough:

> "You know, I don't know why it is I have to listen to all these sexist remarks," I said. "What *is* it about me? Do I ask for these?" He said, "No, it's just that

we know that when we say it you're not taking it personally." And I said, "But do you know that I *really* don't appreciate those remarks? Because I don't feel it's fair that you're giving them to me. Some women deserve them, but I don't think I do!"

Who are these other deserving women?[2] In general, resistance seems highest to women who are competent and confident and make no bones about it: "She was just pushing so much that women could do the job just as well as they could, they were just as strong, just as reliable." These are sentiments that alienate and offend. Here again we see the critical importance of negotiating a satisfactory model of accommodation:

> Like this one summer we had . . . a really gung-ho women's libber. She's really an aggressive person. And she completely turned the guys off. None of the guys liked working with her. They all hated her. . . . Yeah, she was a good worker, if she had a woman boss. Anyway, she was still a good worker with a guy but she complained a lot. And I've found that she's cool when she's working with women, but when she's working with guys she didn't have the same attitude. And that was what turned the guys off toward her, was her attitude.

This fundamental mistake is unforgivable. It weeds out many "uppity women" who eventually quit or are not rehired. One man expresses the dominant sentiment in a familar way: "Hey, when you're in Rome you do as the Romans do. If you want to come up in this organization, lady, you get along with the people."

Whatever the source, resentment is rarely hidden for long. The new-comer may sense disdain or disrespect, may overhear things in passing, or may find herself in a shouting match in the woods one gloomy day—but she will soon recognize the climate of opposition. We have discovered some of the battlegrounds, but what are the weapons? Women are ignored, yelled at, overworked and underestimated. They are as likely to be assigned harder work as to be confined to "polishing the fire truck." They are mocked and taunted, kidded and tested and kidded some more. Training is withheld, performance ratings unfairly biased, and their authority sidestepped. They are an audience for innuendo and the target of rumor and slur; very occasionally they are left on the trail and are assaulted in the woods. An atmosphere of barely concealed resent-ment affects the lives of many more field women than does more overtly hostile action which occasionally raises tears and ruins days. There have been serious confrontations, however, resulting in physical harm, intim-idation, threats to promotion, personal slurs, and relationships so distant and silent that productive work is impossible and each morning more difficult than the last.

Hostility very often takes the form of spiteful comments, callous remarks, and demeaning jokes which insult and patronize women. They are as aggravating and hurtful as they are impossible to avoid or challenge. All day long, one woman's supervisor tells jokes that she considers sexist. When he laughs that women ("and I'm sure he didn't say 'women'—I'm sure he said 'girls'") in the field should be rated by how they "fill out their Smokey-the-Bear T-shirts," she can neither join in the joke nor object with impunity. Women's performance is often greeted with the classic "pretty good for a girl" line: "I've heard it in jest, I've heard it perfectly seriously, I've heard it said just to get me, I've heard it said almost every way."

Women can rarely express the real depth of their hurt and anger over their treatment at work, and pay a high cost for hiding these emotions as a matter of course. A fairly conservative and very young woman, taunted each day about her sexual activity the night before, adopted this false front of necessity: "I just acted very dumb and naive about it, but inside it hurt and made me mad." Watching what happens to friends who rise to the bait, meeting scorn with scorn and anger with anger, silences others. Sometimes women just give up. Trying to please a crew with philosophical objections to women in nontraditional jobs was "like beating my head against the wall. . . . They never thought I was equal, and I knew they never did and they never would." Sometimes it ends in despair:

> [She] was real, real hurt. She told me when she was working for fire as a temporary that the FMO used to come in and give them speeches every day. And she said he made her feel like dirt, just made her feel like she shouldn't be there. Then it got to the point that she didn't even like to come to work. She'd be crying on the way to work because she just knew he was going to— like, everything he said was directed at her.

The Social Control of Resistance

Male hostility can drive woods-working women away, some sooner and more painfully than others. The most successful of them will develop a number of personal and organizational strategies to control male resistance.[3]

Just as men know how to let women know they are unwanted, women also learn to "assert [their] own space." They develop a broad repertoire of strategic personal responses—some dependent on surprise and thus used sparingly, some second nature, and others not so much things to do as ways to be. Whether they rely on humorous or biting rejoinders, unexpected physical response, avoidance, or truce making, the most important lesson is to respond appropriately. Flexibility is critical, whether the problem is lack of job training, unwanted romantic advances, or a matter of gesture and joke. Each woman in the field forges a unique and variable strategy.

Despite variability in situation and response, there are many tactical choices field women share. Humor is an invaluable power resource in the hands of those skilled in quick rejoinder or the elaborate teasing which enlivens the day and "lets everybody relax a little bit." Easier for some than for others, a sense of humor strikes many as essential: "Keep the sense of humor—God, that is *very* important. Half the remarks the guys . . . they don't even think twice about saying it. . . . Half the people don't know that they're saying it. . . . And if you become bitter about those things, God, that could kill you right away and the whole thing wouldn't work out, I'm sure. . . . If you can be humorous and still stick up for yourself . . . "

Women and men alike stress the undercurrent of humor and jibe as the domain in which points are made. More experienced women pass the word: "People are always giving each other shit, and you've just got to be able to give it back." The interviews are dotted with wonderful one-liners composed after the fact and with snappy comebacks (perhaps more polished in the retelling) which reportedly silenced objectionable lines of conversation or innuendo.

Some women are always ready with an effective rejoinder. Accused of being a lesbian one bright morning, one woman simply laughed. The men gathered around expected denial or perhaps embarrassment, but she (in the midst of a secret affair with a co-worker) simply turned to say, "There's one thing for goddamned sure—*you'll* never know for sure." When another woman's co-worker carefully pointed out the insult implicit in a contractor's remark, she sighed—"Yes, I know that, and that's a little lesson that *you* just learned." More amazed than outraged to hear the incredible ("I don't mind if women work . . . , I just don't like the ones who do it for fun") this middle-aged woman of many years experience leaned over the table to say: "Fella—I didn't even call him mister—let me tell you the reason they call it work—w,o,r,k. Don't you know, playing cards, going out dancing . . . , that's what you do for fun. They call this work because that's what it is."

Thinking up witty responses can be "almost like work" for others. One young woman, working with her all-male crew building a trail to a smoldering fire, could think of no witty response when a high-level supervisor turned to her, one of the "girlies" to him, inquiring, "What would your mother say if she knew you were out here?" And there was simply no response possible to the man who remarked, "I really don't want any women on my team, but I understand we have to hire a minority. You're a minority and you're that much better than a nigger. And if we get someplace and have to go down a hole, lady you're going down there."

A very young woman remembers being "scared to death" of a very "tough-looking" man, but when she figured him out he posed no problem. When he grabbed her around her waist, moving toward the boss's office and hollering to all not to disturb them for the day, she simply responded in kind—"Don't bother us! Just call us for lunch." The effect was immediate: "And he just dropped his arm and looked at me like 'Oh, you little shit.' And the whole office got a big kick out of it! Then everybody gets a big laugh out of it and nobody's really put on the spot. It's great fun."

Women also make truces and forge alliances. A woman may defer to male expertise to allay doubts about her attitude and may even accept help she does not need to protect her reputation. This deliberately false demeanor is more common with older men than with younger ones whose motivation strikes more women as less innocent. Some are adept at accepting the opened door with a sweet smile—"Butter them up a little bit, you know . . . , playact like a female at times." On the trail with men they strive for compromise about pace or may agree to meet later at a designated point because of differences in stride; either tactic helps avoid destructive competitiveness.

Male friends and sponsors can be a shield from the worst digs, biased ratings, or destructive gossip, when women share indirectly in their power. Though rare, these strategic alliances are very effective. More common is the support of male co-workers who help discourage the worst behavior in other men by setting the tone. Without encouragement or reaction, the challenge, innuendo, and taunt—"hey, sweetie"—usually subside. In the rare instance of direct intimidation and threat, women know these friendly men can be counted on for concrete help.

Some topics of conversation raise hackles, converting bright mornings into dreary ones, and when they can be singled out, women will avoid them by controlling the conversation. In one instance a garrulous co-worker rambled on each morning about the virtues of the many women he had enjoyed on different continents. Joking protests had no discernible impact, so the woman tried ignoring him and daydreaming during the long drive to the work site. Then she learned how to initiate the conversation "to get him off something like that" by talking about the news on the radio or asking him questions about his career or their profession.

Other women also rely on controlling conversations to avoid uncomfortable sexual connotations. "Learning about their personal life, learning about their wife, about their kids, that sort of thing," makes sexual tension or friction less likely. Many attempt to keep talk at work family centered, just as they dress conservatively, refrain from dating men at work, or cultivate a visible off-work romantic partner to control the sexual atmosphere at work. A calculating naivete occasionally defuses the suggestive context some women find grating; not understanding means not having to respond.

Sheer avoidance of some situations (e.g., partnerships with "roving hands" men or work on crews that are notoriously critical of women) is a most effective short-term tactic no field-going woman overlooks. Walking away, keeping quiet, or simply opting out may not be fair or desirable, but it is often the only alternative. Shouting matches, harangues, and constant criticism are no fun either.

Direct confrontation does sometimes play a role in negotiating relations with hostile or objectionable co-workers. A woman determined "not to be plowed over any more" has no qualms about using her sharp tongue to best advantage and preferably in full view of other men, for "nothing is worse than to have a woman, right in front of everybody, cut them down and show just how stupid they actually are. . . . they're not the big macho male." Using her body more than her tongue works better for another, who delights in turning "old men's faces red" when they persist in remarks designed to embarrass her: "Just by . . . like this one bald guy, just by patting his head! He just blushes, and everybody else thinks it's hysterical. I've gotten everybody there at least once. And it's kind of like . . . they're not too sure if they want to mess with me."

The man who tried this trick may not "mess with" the woman again either: "And one guy, she went up to him one day and he just grabbed her tits. And she said, 'I'll bet you wouldn't do that again,' and he did it again. She kneed him in the balls! She always had a good comeback for everybody. She handles situations a lot differently."

Each woman handles situations differently, reflecting individual resources and interpretation of the situation. Some "dress for success" whenever appropriate, while others concentrate on learning the bureaucratic ground rules and how to "play by them—but you have to know them better than they do or you won't make it." Others emphasize their own strength and fearlessness: "I'll fight off any guy that tries to touch me. I'm just not afraid of men, I guess, in general . . . , and I let them know it."

Despite their differences, most agree that a thick skin is essential for women now and a defensive attitude only an invitation to trouble: "But people who start working with the attitude that 'this is the male role and I'm going to have to fight all the way'—they're *going* to have to fight all the way. . . . They're 'in the male role' and they're going to have to prove themselves, and they just are continually battling, trying to put up a show, trying to meet somebody else's expectations, that they themselves set."

Controlling male resistance means learning to be discriminating. Many people may "feel that you shouldn't be there—and some people will be able to do something about it and others can't," observes one experienced woman. Some men may respond to the "coy, sweet, little innocent know-nothing," while others can be "hit head-on." Flexibility is critical, even if it feels like weakness or uncertainty.

A primary challenge facing women is learning to anticipate repercussions accurately in devising personal responses to hostile men. On some crews, objecting to dirty magazines or sexy talk is tantamount to asking for more. Plain speaking can clarify and reinforce vast differences, leading to isolation and alienation: "It became real hard, because I was always alone . . . , and it got real uncomfortable, going to work every day." And the jokes never stopped. The reputation of being a troublemaker, divisive, or "hard to get along with"—euphemisms for outspoken women confident of their ability—destroys some women.

Direct confrontation, verbal or physical, entails more risk than avoidance, compromise, or other tactics. "Lots of times I don't handle it well at all, because they want me to get mad and so I get mad," one woman admits. Being fast on the draw and quick to take offense may jeopardize physical safety in the woods. At any rate, men are always easier to tackle as individuals: "I can never relate to them as a group, period—because it scares me, it frightens me, you know? There's too much energy going on there."

Women of experience pass on similar advice to those who will follow: "Tolerance, probably, would be my advice to the working woman. Tolerate it but don't let them step on you. . . . You get flies with sugar better than with vinegar, you know? I mean, you don't have to go overboard on the sugar."

But there are limits to tolerance. For one woman, who was firmly convinced that "when there are that many men in the organization, you're really stupid to try to buck anything—you only make trouble for yourself," the limit was passed when coffee-break chat turned to rape, and the men chimed in with the familiar victim-blaming refrain. Others draw the line when career plans are threatened or when family life is touched by conflict at work.

With time and perspective and in conjunction with others, they learn not to take offense easily and when to stand firm: "And you also have to have an understanding about some men, where they are coming from. It's new for them too, and you can't just go in and radically expect them to accept you immediately. You *do* have to prove yourself to a certain point. But when it gets to that point beyond—that's when I get mad! I've done it—don't you believe I can do it?!"

Women advise others to be strong and fearless, assertive of their rights yet sensitive to male ego and tradition, quick with their tongues but slow to anger. They should draw on the strength of friends and sponsors and their own self-confidence, learn to control conversations and make truces—above all, learn tolerance and its limits. It is a tall order:

> Don't go in with any set ideas. Don't think that you know how it's going to be, because it's not, and don't think you know how to react in a given situation because everything is going to be different. . . . There's reasons why people do everything, and if you don't know the reason you can't really get down on a person for something. Everything's an action and reaction, so if you come off being really hard, you're going to get hard responses, or if you come off being really childish and silly and typical—quote—"female"— you're going to get it back. Everything that I've put in, I've gotten back.

Feminist Friends

This account focuses on women's relations with the men they meet at work in the woods. By and large, the women speaking here form their closest and most enduring relationships with those working alongside— and these are nearly always male co-workers and bosses. While the Forest Service tries to avoid isolating a solo woman on an all-male crew, carefully placing at least two women on most crews, these women generally do not form a distinct subgroup. Rather, because they work with more experienced workers for informal training and because women's interests and abilities are rarely identical, most work closely with men. Many things divide women field workers from one another, whether or not they work on the same crew—their different backgrounds and skills, their styles and goals, and the relations they typically forge with the men and women around them.

Yet as newcomers to the occupation, the crew, and often the community, women are naturally very aware of other women in similar situations, in another department or a neighboring district or a different field crew. As they spoke about their experiences integrating woods work, many wondered aloud how others were faring, wishing they could know the other women nearby a bit better. As we have seen, though they are yet so few, women field workers have a profound influence on each other indirectly, though they may meet only rarely.

Woods-working women may see more of the clerical women in the offices to which they return each afternoon. Interaction between indoor and outdoor women is rarely simple or easy. There is a feeling that indoor-working women, more often in dresses and curls, look down on "mannish" women whose preference is for outdoor work and who easily accept the routine dirt and sweat and discomfort of it. Some seem to question their motivation for wanting to work so intimately with men. Clerical women sometimes resent field-working women whose unskilled labor (piling brush or shoveling dirt) pays them so much more than does the Forest Service administrative and secretarial work. The new women workers also have a different way of acting around the men at work: "Sometimes it's not very good. A lot of times they're in dead-end, low-paying jobs, plus there is . . . if you've been working with the men for a long time, you're at a better level of rapport with them—the buddy thing. And that is a threat to the way they relate to the men, in their feminine level, in the office."

Far from being "different kinds" of women, as men often argue, indoor and outdoor women work in two fundamentally different situations, with different skills, priorities, and demands. Many field workers were once clerical, and many clerical workers are eager to tag along on field excursions whenever possible. Recognizing this interest, more than one field woman makes a point of taking interested clerical women along if possible and helping them find other chances to get out occasionally, to encourage and "to repay her." Sometimes close friendships form between women in different parts of the organization, and many field workers feel secretaries are "cheering us on," perhaps even anticipating the day when there will be women as well as men directing their work. They are able to help each other in concrete ways occasionally with job hints and inside knowledge and by sharing experiences with difficult men. Other women, however, carefully limit interaction with nonprofessional or indoor-working women. One woman explains why she feels it important to adopt this stance: "As far as the way I was perceived, in the eyes of the people I worked with—the engineers, the geologist, other people—being categorized with those women would be detrimental. They would never speak to those women in the kind of terms . . . that I wanted for me. And therefore that was not to my advantage, and so I didn't really foster those relationships."

Coming together as women, whether in the office or in the field, is not easy at this stage. Yet women's support of each other as women is a key resource in the social control of male resistance. When women around the districts do meet to share problems and strategies, hopes and anxieties, they begin to break down the isolation and alienation of the token minority. Sometimes they unite as self-consciously feminist allies—and feminists in the Forest Service seem to find each other wherever they are. This group of women includes very many strikingly independent women with unusual lives—women who drove logging trucks twenty years ago or who took animal trapping jobs at nineteen. As a whole, they are outspoken, self-sufficient, and quite prepared to fight for their rights when necessary. "Field-going women are a gutsy bunch—they fight for everything they get," one says with pride. They have the personal confidence to deal directly with powerful men, and many will fight for issues affecting women generally.

They certainly do not all define themselves as feminists, however, nor as radicals or insurgents. Yet they share at a minimum a sense of respect for women as a group. Feminists among them are sisters to each other rather than to the male crew. They may not always prefer to work together (though many do) nor even see much of each other (though on several districts feminists regularly gather on evenings or weekends). They share some sense of the history of women and have a common commitment to united action to improve the future of all working women.

Yet in the field and in the office, feelings and circumstance intervene to muddy things. Women are divided by conflicting models for relating to men and by different expectations of themselves and other women; relations between women are as complex as relations between women and men. The help women need in dealing with male hostility comes most naturally and significantly from other women as they share advice and information, give solace and encouragement, and simply take the time to listen. But a bond does not come automatically. In forging alliances, women field workers look first to other women but sometimes find themselves relying instead on male co-workers, insightful supervisors, and concerned outsiders or family members. Feminists point out the untapped potential for meaningful cooperation among field-going women, and the many obstacles to it. One frustrated activist sums up: "But the reason the system doesn't work, for women or for anybody, is because like hires like and is allowed to. The second thing is because our input doesn't get into the system. And the third thing is because we don't get together. Women just don't get together enough. We don't talk together well enough, and we don't trust each other enough, and we don't work for each other."

Still, there is a spirit of great ferment and change now. For some women the very experience of becoming a Forest Service field worker is a radicalizing experience, making them feminists where *Ms.* magazine failed. As more women enter the field and confront the same problems of access, blocked mobility and stereotyping, denial of training and female authority, the feminist networks will likely increase in strength and import.

Organizational Resources

Conflict between women and men generally remains just below the surface, coloring daily interaction but not forcing public management. When hostility does suddenly become public and affects the quality of work, supervisors must deal overtly with it—meetings will be called and grievances aired, work assignments changed and warnings issued.

Some women will write formal letters of complaint rather than confront a manhandler directly. Others work only in the background, relying on sponsors and friends to make their case for them. Another woman will quit before she breathes a word of what happened to anyone. But the group also includes women who stride directly into their unit manager's office to say that they will not work one season longer as temporaries, or to insist on their right to attend project fires, or to ask for help with persistent Romeos or manhandlers.

One source of power that women have not fully realized is the strategy of abandoning the personal realm and going public—or threatening to. Like other workers, women in the field with concrete job grievances can do more than simply grin and bear it.

The Federal Women's Program is a vehicle for defining and communicating problems facing women, and it has filled an invaluable role in data collection and focusing management attention on women's issues. It is chiefly important as an organizing vehicle bringing women throughout the organization together. Its impact varies widely among the districts. In some places women are unaware of much more than the initials of the group. A monthly newsletter and the many meetings involved consume the available energy quickly. District representatives sometimes recommend housing prospects to newcomers or lobby for work gloves in women's sizes; at other times they take on issues like sexual harassment, documenting cases for management review.

Career-planning sessions, lunch-bag seminars on topics of interest, or a chance to learn the faces and names of other women around the district are all needed. This opportunity was lacking when many women came on board and it makes a difference—a difference perhaps too little appreciated by newer women, some feel. Its primary benefit may lie in bringing women together: "Well, the neat thing that came out of it wasn't the career development, it was the closeness that the women developed."

During its short history the program has engaged the energies of the original activists nearly to exhaustion, and apparently it has not yet inspired a second generation. Little work time is allocated to those who would like more active roles. Other women shy away because of the feminist reputation attached to activists; FWP representatives must occasionally face male co-workers and supervisors as adversaries in advocating the interests of women. To some the program seems irrelevant: "[It's] more of a resource center, kind of a supportive group, and I guess that's why I never got very involved in it. I've never felt like I needed their support. . . . I've always felt like if I wanted something, I went after it—and I'm so loud and pushy, they usually give it to me just to shut me up!"

Both critics and supporters agree that the program could do more. Some feel that its domination by indoor-working women keeps it from an activist role; certainly the functions and meetings are more difficult for field workers to attend, especially during the busy field season. In some districts only permanent women may take time off to attend FWP functions, and temporary workers are categorically excluded. In part because of skepticism about the FWP, local chapters of Federally Employed Women are being organized to galvanize feminist concerns.

Complaints of sex discrimination are pursued not through the Federal Women's Program or the union but primarily through the equal employment opportunity counseling system. While the FWP may be important in other ways (i.e., in establishing a claim to bureaucratic equity or in providing a needed "safety valve" for the disaffected), it is very rarely used to explore the complex issues of gender so apparent in conversations with women field workers.

EEO counselors tend to be men of fairly high status who hold their positions (through appointment, volunteering, or peer election) for more than a year. Most claim they are in touch with the undercurrents of rumor and gossip around the district, where problems are first aired; with male counselors and female complainants, however, this contact may not be easy. At any rate, counselors are rarely consulted in their formal capacity. Half of the consultations reported were with men; women seeking help were half indoor and half outdoor workers and three times as often were temporary workers. Some unit counselors have yet to counsel anyone, though others are widely known as helpful and influential men. Counselors are mandated to attempt informal conflict resolution but also to facilitate formal complaints if necessary. They seem to have succeeded; in all, they report just one instance of a formal complaint fully pursued to resolution.

Management affects women's inclination to make problems public, if only to the local counselor. Unit managers and counselors sometimes speak as if the system were a bother but were organizationally useful to forestall scandal and keep conflict private. Some male managers, supervisors, and workers object to bureaucratic management of what seem like private issues.

One manager insists, "If you take an adverse action against a woman you had better be able to document it," so certain is he that women regularly file complaints of discrimination. Several, indeed, have been implicated personally in complaints during their careers. Occasionally the threat of formal action is an effective weapon for women, though rarely does it surface above the realm of the offhand joke. There have been instances, however, of threatened formal complaints (e.g., advising a ranger of intent to file should essential training continue to be denied), which may contribute to the free-floating defensiveness about women's pursuit of their interests.

Asked about pursuing grievances, one woman sums up a very common feeling: "Well, if it had been a dangerous situation, I probably would have—or something completely intolerable, you know, like getting raped." With respect to more tolerable problems, most field-going women decline. They mention in passing various instances which might have been formally pursued but were not, for the personal cost is usually judged too great.

Going public with a complaint, beginning with a visit to the counselor, results principally in notoriety and in public conflict regarding the legitimacy of the complaint and complainant. Women report losing male and female friends, watching former supporters turn against them, facing threats to their job or promotion or future employment with the Forest Service. Conflicts involving organizational superiors (as most do) make women especially vulnerable to repercussions. Their stories may be disbelieved, denied, or ridiculed. "It went all the way to the forest supervisor" in one case, "because when you come to get butt, they start covering butt, all the way to the top, and they don't care how wrong they are." The frustrations of paperwork and endless meetings deter some, but women also fear for their safety as the daily atmosphere at work deteriorates. Though very rare, fear is more effective in silencing women than ostracism, blacklisting, or threats. ("You know, your stock went down when you went in to talk to him," one supervisor said to a woman seeking counseling.) A woman with experience looks back: "And I just knew that if some idiot out there on the crew thought 'Hey, we'll get rid of her,' I could get seriously injured or really something happen to me. I wasn't really sure at that point who supported me and who didn't. I got the hell out of there. I quit, because it got dangerous."

As in sexual harassment cases, those who "make waves" can expect challenge from both women and men. As friends become remote and strangers hostile, women pursuing cases of sexual discrimination wonder about their decision to go public. Those nearby do not wonder—they know by observation that nothing short of catastrophe will make them take that irrevocable step. For those who do continue, the end is always uncertain:

> But if you've ever talked to the EEO counselor . . . , most of them just really don't care, and they're kind of nervous about a lot of it. And some of them try and there's nothing they can do. You know, "Well, that's the way it is." And they get more pressure from the top to shut it up because the ranger doesn't want any of this let out because it's bad for *his* record, the forest supervisor has *his* record, and so on.

The many obstacles to linking private troubles and organizational issues repress the airing of many issues of equity in the workplace. Ultimately, discrimination grounded in the nature of the workplace and organizational management of female newcomers is reduced to the nebulous terrain of personality conflict and private dispute. In dealing with manhandlers and restrictive job assignments alike, women continue to act alone, though their repertoire of interpersonal tactics is rarely appropriate to all the issues which arise as careers progress and situations change.

Many share the sentiment, if not the conclusions of one frustrated speaker who commented:

> They put women out in field situations which are very dangerous, and they don't prepare those intermediate supervisors—the ones that have to deal with them, the crew bosses. They don't *talk* to those dudes. They spend millions of dollars on these damn assertiveness programs and human rights . . . but they don't tell those people on the ground how to get along with each other. And they don't have somebody there, checking up on them, interviewing those women and those men, saying, "Are there any problems?" Somebody that knows what the problems are. Because people say,

"No, there's no problem, but somebody just threw me off a mountain yesterday." And all the normal manager wants to hear is "No, there's no problem," and that's all he hears, right? But they've got situation after situation.

Protecting the low profile they feel is essential to acceptance at work is the overriding goal of most field-going women. Without change in the atmosphere and politics of grievance they are unlikely to alter their commitment to personal conflict management. As individuals and as a group, they are too vulnerable—and the risk is too great—to tackle institutional solutions to institutional conflict. They much prefer personal strategies individually fashioned to deal with opposition from men at work. If only they could, they would all sidle in as gracefully as this woman: "I don't feel that my doing [my work] is a big to-do, so I don't get a lot of people noticing what's going on, and it just happens. You've slid in there and you're alongside them, and they just didn't know what was going on! And it's too late, because they *like* you now."

Patterns of Change

Neither acceptance nor resistance is a stable category, nor are the two always clear. The suspicious crew boss can become a friend, and just as easily a powerful, perhaps embittered ex-lover. There can be no neat categorizations in this or any other social world between good guys and bad, the fair or unfair. Patterns of change structure the daily work world as significantly as patterns of resistance and acceptance.

Initial skepticism and hostility can change in many ways to eventual nonchalance or even to companionship. It can happen even to the most unsuspecting, and unexpectedly. The man who ostentatiously remarked to all nearby how much he enjoyed one woman's breasts ("Thank you," she said, and walked away) later became a good friend. A young man unhappy about his assignment to a mixed-sex fire crew soon discovered he enjoyed having women around: "A woman with muscles is like driving a sports car instead of an old junker."

Acceptance can develop as part of a gradual normalizing process during weeks, seasons, or years. Working with women in extraordinary places and ways loses its strangeness as the organization, district, and individuals all gain experience and perspective. The period of testing and proving and protecting eventually comes to an end as tolerances and routines are established. Language, for instance, quickly changes when women join in with a resounding curse which echoes through the woods and the organization itself. The bathroom arrangement is questioned and resolved early on, and this part of the working day is normalized. Competence is demonstrated, and men cease worrying that they must be "nursemaids" monthly to their female co-workers. As they and their families become known around the community, women feel more comfortable sharing social activities into which they initially introduce a certain tension. Through the afternoon drink, the barbecue, and the Christmas party they begin to know the wives and lovers of the men at work. As work routines are established and faces become familiar, everyone relaxes—at least until the next newcomer arrives upon the scene.

Women with experience grow stronger and less defensive. They learn when they are being tested and how to be discriminating in their response. They also begin to understand what men want—an accomplishment as important and difficult as learning to maneuver a split-axle truck or run a fertilizer-spreading machine. One woman remembers an important moment:

> Every once in a while after work we'd go have drinks with the guys. And I got talking with the guys and all the guys I talked to said, "Gee, you're the first woman I've liked working with." At first I thought, "Wow, that's neat." Then I thought, "Wait a minute, why?" So I asked them—"Why? Why should I be any different than any other woman?" And they said, "Well, for one thing, you don't complain. For a second thing, you pull your share of the work." And I got to noticing it's true. Because it's really easy to let yourself fall into that trap. [For example, she was run ragged trying to follow three men in excellent condition when she first began.] And so they said, "Oh, just stand on the survey line and take notes." And I said, "No, that isn't fair. I should do my share." And they said, "Oh, come on." And it bugged me. . . . [So she talked it over with them.] "It bugs me because I don't think I'm doing my share." And he says, "Look, I know I'm in better shape than you are. And I want those cross-sections done!" And I guess I was so worried that they were thinking that I couldn't do it because I was a woman, and that didn't—they didn't think that way.

Sudden conversion is also possible. Men originally skeptical if not antagonistic have had miraculous changes of heart. All it took in one case was a bottle of wine and a long conversation in the truck as they waited out a thunderstorm. The "obnoxious turkey" who seemed to hate women needed only proof positive of one woman's seriousness about her work to become a good buddy. Even a man who deliberately felled trees dangerously close to her (or so she felt) later became a best friend. And the young professional man who vowed to the ranger he would never work with women eventually came to see one woman "almost like a mother." In many cases all that is necessary is a chance for women to prove their ability, and a good forest fire or an especially grueling traverse can do the trick.

This theme of conversion, whether in a blinding flash of insight and communication or trial by fire, makes fast friends of avowed enemies, and women proudly report on every instance. In fire fighting especially, women speak of men's new-found respect for the women of the woods. This example is from the early days of integration, when an all-woman crew was detailed to help fight fire. The crew of middle-aged women reported to an unsuspecting fire boss:

> And I stepped out of the rig, held my hand out, and told him [who they were], and fell over my butt! Which made a really good impression. I got up and shook off—all these fat ladies piling out of the rig. And he's just standing there. . . . "What am I going to *do* with them? God, we've got a fire going!" Well, we worked for him for two days, and when we got all done, he come and shook all of our hands and told us to meet him at the bar whenever we got through, he'd buy us a drink, and that he was really pleased he'd got the opportunity to work with us—we did real good.

The Forest Service prides itself on a shared purpose and "family" spirit of this kind, with workers inclined to working hard together and celebrating too. Districts vary in sociability, as in their tendency to segregate by rank, with separate social lives for warehouse and office workers, or overhead and temporaries, for instance. Most women are as much a part of the socializing and intimacy as they desire, and male co-workers and supervisors (and their families) are usually eager to befriend them. Very few women work in an atmosphere of unrelenting hostility—although the air may be charged and volatile, it is as often friendly as not.

Women field workers lucky enough to enjoy both their work and co-workers speak in glowing terms of their relationships at work. They describe bosses as friends and co-workers as brothers and sisters. People are "just as concerned about what's going on at home as we are about what's going on at the job," or as another woman put it, "it's a lot of laughter, and not only work support but family support." They share troubles, decisions, drinks, and gossip in a friendly atmosphere which unites groups otherwise very diverse.

Women value accepting men who give them time to develop physical condition and skills and who challenge and trust their growing ability. They "treat you like you're worth knowing—like you're as intelligent as they." They will consider strengths as well as weaknesses, give women the benefit of the doubt and stand up for them if necessary. They are trustworthy and not slackers themselves or inclined to "play games" with their female co-workers. They are men to whom women can be comfortably close.

Women and men alike report that when all goes well they enjoy work friendships greatly enhanced for being grounded in common interests and experiences. The uncertainties generated by stereotyping, paternalism, testing and proving, and sexual themes resolve eventually into easy ways of being close and real satisfaction in doing a good day's work together. Both women and men are amazed they can talk so freely with one another. And always, of course, they are "just kidding around." Heading home after a day of slash burning, a man and a woman who were friends enacted the following scenario for the benefit of those nearby. In a stage voice, he pronounced: "'God, I'm sure glad to see you getting out of there. Fighting fires is not a place for a woman—this is man's work.' 'God yes, I'll be *so* happy to get home to my kitchen. I'm going to go home and bake some bread and do my dishes.' And one of the other guys says, 'How do you get away talking to her like that?' Oh, we have a real good relationship!"

While not all women are willing to give hostile men the benefit of the doubt, most hope with time for gradual conversion and remain cautiously optimistic: "Most of them are real intelligent and, I feel, *trying* to accept women. They're coming from a place where they haven't . . . they're not used to having women there, and they're trying to adjust to it, as well as us trying to adjust to being there. I would say, as a general rule, they're pretty good about it."

With a few notable exceptions, male co-workers and bosses are both the source and solution to problems, friend and foe at once. Men draw lines of resistance at different points and times, and women define and press their case very differently. The partner who welcomes and gladly trains a woman for routine work may become her outspoken opponent when she wants to accompany the crew to a project fire or aspires to a supervisory position, for example. The same crew which laughs through the day, meeting for a drink both Friday and Monday after work ("because a lot of us haven't seen each other over the weekend") may on occasion be torn apart by struggle over any of the issues reviewed here. As routinely as tempers flare, respect and confidence and even affection emerge and critical alliances are forged.

A peculiar form of male acceptance is striking. Some men come to prefer working on mixed-sex crews or offices and value the intimacy with women afforded by their work. But their reasons for enjoying women co-workers are often traditional. They appreciate having women near because everyone "cleans up their act a little bit," and more varied topics of conversation are possible. Some stress women's advantage as workers on the crew; they find women self-motivated and enthusiastic, willing to put thought as well as muscle into their work. Their presence keeps some men working and a little sexual competition may get the day's work done faster. How can they resist "just a busy little worker," especially when she is also good-looking and occasionally brings "treats" like brownies to work? Women co-workers are seen as group "morale boosters" who also provide men with "ego support" and "break the monotony" of the all-male group. They are "so much fun" to have around when they appear sexually naive and willingly laugh at themselves. And ultimately, women in the field are simply "better to look at." Most of all, what men like is women who agree with them, who understand and accept their conception of women in the field. The "ladylike buddy" is a powerful model of accommodation smoothing the way for those who can use it successfully.

For these and other reasons, many men are content to work with women, and why not? The portrait they sketch does not challenge traditional conceptions of femininity or gender relations. In the face of this most nontraditional work setting—where women in rain gear slide down slippery slopes to tube seedlings or to collect carcasses from traps— the critical elements of gender relations are reinforced. Women's presence provides the opportunity to affirm traditional relations while preserving male control over key areas of work and privilege and workplace culture—with hard work and brownies too.

Acceptance does not come easily or unconditionally. Male workers do set conditions and erect barriers, and the integration of women field workers is predicated on conformity to these implicit terms of entry. Those women who are "easygoing" or determined enough to adapt eventually achieve the conditional acceptance within which friendship and respect blossom.

Trends and Possibilities

Male resistance to women woods workers, and how successfully it is managed, transformed, or muted into conditional acceptance, pose important limits to integration. There are other limits rooted empirically in the larger context of change. The halting entry of women into all-male sanctuaries of work proceeds in a historical, organizational, and political-economic context. How many tanker foremen wear braids or male workers share lunch with hard-hatted women now? How many will do so a decade from now? These questions touch on the national economy and on the politics of affirmative action, trends within forestry and the Forest

Service, and the ambitions and family decisions of women workers. Each deserves attention in analyzing factors hindering and facilitating the integration of field work.[4]

Organizational Directions

Two trends demand attention for their impact on the future of women field workers—bureaucratization and professionalization, and the economic squeeze slowing the trend toward specialization.

Old-timers cherish their memories, but the day is long past when district rangers made daily work assignments as easily in tree planting, road construction, or fence building and when only the assignment to office work surprised workers with diverse outdoor skills. Lacking both necessary equipment and expertise, the agency now depends on others for a wide range of labor. Tree planting, log scaling, precommercial thinning, road and trail construction, cone picking, fire fighting, and other traditional tasks are increasingly contracted out to the private sector, dramatically altering the nature of Forest Service employment. Contract administration and inspection increase in importance as government workers apply detailed agency job specifications while others take to the woods to do the job. Management-oriented professional degrees are more valuable as report writing, supervision, and contract writing and inspection grow in importance. Because contractors relieve the agency of the responsibilities of labor management and help reduce the requisite number of federal job ceilings, the trend is likely to continue.

The implications are mixed for female newcomers to forestry. For professional women the discernible shift from hard labor to the "soft" domain of contract supervision deemphasizes physique, long viewed as disabling, while drawing on enabling strengths in verbal and written communication. Nonprofessional women trained as log scalers or timber cruisers may have to follow the work to the private sector, where their prospects for employment and acceptance are bleaker. Differences of social and organizational class can only be exacerbated. The young woman thrilled with her hard-won forest technician degree from the local community college may join others in her family on welfare when her seasonal work in animal control is phased out—even as opportunities increase for professional women with biology degrees inspecting contract work in animal control.

The federal budget crunch also affects women field workers directly. The historical trend toward specialized staff positions created jobs for professional women, but these opportunities will shrink as the agency loses its expensive specialists. Combining the geologist and engineer into one engineering geologist or mining engineer job doubly disadvantages women by virtue of underrepresentation in both male-dominated fields. Budgetary cuts at the federal level may first affect public services in recreation work (e.g., campground and trail maintenance), areas considered more appropriate for women field workers. The loss of publicly funded programs like the Youth Conservation Corps also affects women with backgrounds in youth work and recreation hired to manage these nontraditional crews. Certainly, continued retrenchment in federal employment increases the already stiff competition for permanent field jobs and raises the educational ante just as women begin their careers.

Will the future bring a more secure place for women field workers, or will things soon "revert back," with men resuming their monopoly over forest work? This question was put by an old-timer more indifferent than hostile to the entry of women into his line of work. He and others look to the day the national craze for integration passes into distant memory and normalcy returns to the assignment and selection of work. The question is presently unanswerable but important. It affects not only the lives and futures of those touched by affirmative action in the Forest Service but the future of the organization and of field work.

Some feel that in the long run, sexual integration in field work will be "civilizing." A new maturity may follow sexual sharing of work and workplace. Referring to "sexy" calendars in office and warehouse, one woman wondered aloud why women tolerate at work what many would resent in their own homes: "Is that what we're going to do—treat them as little boys all the time? When do they grow up, or is it only women that have to grow up?"

Some anticipate new workplace rights for both sexes, though the new rights will have been inspired initially by women field workers. These include adequate shower facilities at project fire camps; work clothes reflecting differences in size and build; career counseling for all those who need or desire it; separate toilets at fire camps, as in "normal society"; and more flexible policies concerning family hiring, mandatory overtime, or promotional transfers. Some women environmentalists see women forest workers as a positive force in the eventual redirection of the agency back to "really taking care of the woods."

Despite traditional patterns and limitations, even small steps toward the sexual integration of field work are meaningful and full of promise. The sheer presence of women working shoulder to shoulder with men in the woods challenges deeply held convictions and raises questions difficult to push aside. In private moments and ways men and women of all backgrounds reconsider what work means to them, what qualities masculinity and femininity engage, and what they hope the future will bring.

This book can only hint at the shape of that future. One young woman, however, has a clear and inspirational vision of the long-term impact of sexual integration in field work:

> But eventually I think it would be really fantastic, just like any other field, any other social situation, professional or anything. When there's equal input of male and female, you get the best of both. That's the way, you know—everything evolves. You don't go for the worst, you go for the best. So I think a lot of the characteristics that I'm finding that annoy me about my male counterparts would . . . soften. . . . They would realize that it's all right to have certain characteristics—it doesn't demean them. . . . And [women] would stand up for themselves. They would get more confident. They would have more strength—inner and outer.

Her optimism is shared by many men as well. This manager speaks from a career spanning three decades: "I think it's awful nice to see . . . the people working together. Because it's more *natural*. Men go home and live with women, and why should they be by themselves on the job, you know? This is where you spend most of your life, why not enjoy it? And I think men and women enjoy being with each other, so why not?"

Others share a vision of the future in which "the women's jobs and the men's jobs, so to speak, just don't hold water anymore," and the "be like a man or be like a woman" syndrome is no longer compelling at work. They hope for a day when gender "neither enhances nor detracts" from individuality or work status.

These glimmers of an uncertain future are as far as this study can venture in outlining future employment prospects for women field workers. The implications are mixed, but certainly both worker and work will continue to change as the Forest Service adjusts to women in field work.

Woods-Working Women: "They're Going to See Me Again"

Many changes lie ahead for the Forest Service. Women in positions of authority over large numbers of men or in direct competition with high-status men will test the commitment to integration. Working with larger numbers of women, with more high-status women, and with more activist feminists will pose new problems for male co-workers and supervisors.

Nepotism policy will loom large on the future agenda for workplace equity. When women cannot work, because a spouse or family member is employed by the Forest Service, families lose valued and necessary incomes, marriages are reluctantly postponed, and careers are short-circuited or abandoned. Many know of former field-working women eager but unable to work because their husbands have jobs in the same district or department. The policy is broadly interpreted by unit managers and reflects both labor supply and personal prejudice. One manager accepts all but direct supervisory relations between spouses or family members, while another automatically excludes spouses from any district job.

Discretion in interpreting nepotism policy can benefit women. For example, when one ranger learned of a wife's expertise with the computerized Timber Resources Inventory (TRI) system, he suddenly reconsidered his hasty denial of a job simply because her husband had transferred into the district. Very rarely do skilled women languish at home when managers are sympathetic to the problems of dual-career families. In remote areas, male workers' wives have traditionally worked as clericals in the same district when their labor is needed, as it often is. Problems can only intensify as women branch out from clerical work and more field-working women take partners and begin to manage dual careers.

Other problems are raised by Forest Service couples—and it is important to remember that one-third of those interviewed live with or date Forest Service men. Partners' respective needs for job experience and promotion are often different. Yet the practice of joining transfer with promotion assumes a single career and mobile family. For instance, one couple met while she was beginning her career and he had applied for transfer into a GS-9 position. Early years of their marriage were marked by long commutes, first for one and then for the other. For her career progress they now reluctantly contemplate a temporary hiatus in Alaska, where labor shortages may bring faster promotion. For the present, beginning a family is out of the question.

Women in non-Forest Service dual-earner families also complain of lost opportunities because of immobility. As one woman concluded, a job off-forest meant possible promotion and a needed change, but also a very long daily commute—and while "I might have a house . . . , I don't think I'd have a husband if I did that." Dual-career couples feel prepared to "bend as necessary" to manage both careers. A meaningful affirmative action program helps by examining the implications of organizational policy and tradition for workers' family lives.

The women in this study represent a particular demographic group and moment in the life cycle. Of those not married or living with men, few are concerned now about potential conflict between family and job. Those just a bit older do wonder increasingly about the complications of career, romance, and family. As a group they tend not to have or to want families. This pattern may change as women and their marriages mature. In the long run there is no reason to suppose the labor force might not include middle-aged field-working mothers, just as it now includes middle-aged, field-working fathers.[5]

For all couples, but especially those jointly employed by the Forest Service, there will be new and pressing issues as women and men bring family and work worlds closer, including nursing mothers in the field, granting maternity or paternity leaves during short field seasons, offering day-care facilities in remote areas, and modifying the fire-fighting obligations of parents of young children. Perhaps project fire camps, for instance, will eventually include portable nurseries. One man with many years in fire control and the Forest Service acknowledges that he "can very easily see us taking the day-care centers with us"—adding only, "I hope I retire by then!"

These issues raised by lifelong field careers for women reinforce widespread feelings of male workers and managers that women workers are transitory. And some will be, especially at the entry level of seasonal technician. Many women and men at this level share complaints about working in the heart of the "bumbling bureaucracy"—which sometimes seems to specialize in "multiple use mismanagement." The woman planning to "take this training and run—I'm tired of working for peanuts" has many male counterparts. Many things "just sort of eat away at" pleasure in their work, from restrictions on political activism or lack of communication between departments to some co-workers' relaxed attitudes to work (e.g., "don't, and say you did"). One lifelong critic of government work and workers is mildly horrified to find herself "involved with it up to my eyeballs." Many feel their potential is neglected and share the complaints of the overeducated and underemployed. This woman's misgivings, if not her degree, are widely shared: "Here I am, I've got a master's degree and I'm cleaning restrooms. . . . I was really despondent, had considered going back to an old boyfriend and stuff like that—you know you're low then!"

For women there are also other sources of disillusionment and frustration and problems they face alone. For some the possible health risk of work near herbicides is not worth the limited reward; others lose interest in sustained rigorous physical labor. Constant struggle for training, supervisory experience, or the keys to the truck discourages women field workers too. The daily encounter with the "good old boy" atmosphere has some planning different futures. Most women know of others who have tried field work and for these and other reasons have moved on to other jobs. They wonder if they too should begin to look elsewhere.

The conditional acceptance we have seen most women field workers able to achieve is not always enough. The limits seem harsher to some than to others. One woman accepts her "different purpose" on the crew, compensating for physical limitations with "moral support" and confidential listening. Another finds the limits depressing: "There's only one thing I've found. You can't be one of the guys, you just can't. There's no way. They're not going to let you." It is a great loss when one woman leaves the Forest Service through sheer despair of ever becoming genuinely a part of the family at work, sharing fully in satisfying labor.

Traditionalists comfort themselves that "most women don't want to spend the next thirty or forty years hauling hose up out of a unit." Or do they? Nine of the women interviewed (including several in their twenties) intend if possible to retire in the Forest Service, and the great majority feel committed to outdoor work of some kind. One-quarter of the temporary and one-half of the permanent women plan careers in the Forest Service; others hope to work outdoors in other ways, perhaps trying private industry, nursery work, or subsistence farming. While sometimes this commitment reflects immobility or economic need, the Forest Service offers many the kind of work they have dreamed of for years.

The most determined will stay. They value their work highly and see their lives changing in ways they never anticipated. They will not easily give up hard-won jobs in the woods for a return to the office or factory or restaurant. High salaries compensate for involuntary overtime, growing physical strength rewards daily weariness, and the excitement of new skills more than warrants the occasional struggle it takes to exercise them. Even the rain cannot deter those fascinated by their new jobs: "But once you're out, you start working, and you warm up. And you hear the rain pattering on your hard hat and the woods have a really nice smell, and there's all kinds of little fungus and stuff growing. It's really pretty. And the mist comes in."

This woman has no laundry list of helpful hints for those who follow, but she speaks for many women when she concludes:

> I think you just do it. But I think you have to do it aggressively at this point. Hopefully in the future you won't. You'll be able to just do it, as you do any other job, and not watch every single move you make. . . . And I think that we'll get there eventually. Well, I'm hoping the women are going to stick it out here. There are a lot of real good women that are making a good show.

The future of this woman and the many like her in these two study forests is contingent on no single factor but resides in the overall context of women and their work in the Forest Service. A continued strong commitment to women field workers at all levels of the organization is vital. Yet in the long run the more decisive arena is the daily one of intimacy and confrontation, as women and men tromp through brush together, share lunch and jokes as well as insults, and trade skills and confidences. This is center stage in the sharing of work and in learning new ways to live and work together. Here all are pioneers in change, and even on the bleakest days women remain convinced that their future is bright: "To see the sun coming up, and the birds starting to sing, and you're way out in the middle of nowhere—it was worth it, all of it."

If the obstacles are severe, the rewards are also great, and women feel equal to the task. The challenge to the Forest Service is to nourish this spirit and all the promise it holds.

Summary

Many factors influence the acceptance of these women pioneers in forestry, imposing limits to the successful integration of the work. This chapter considered patterns in male hostility and the spirit of accepting men, and the many paths between the two.

When necessary, women use various personal and organizational resources to parry male opposition. Social control of male resistance is largely the responsibility of individual women, whose most effective strategies privatize conflict. Such tactics as humor, physical affront, truce, and alliance help most avoid making their problems public. The repercussions of pursuing private troubles as organizational issues deter many women from fully using formal avenues of support and grievance. In the hands of committed women, the Federal Women's Program is a potentially powerful resource. Presently, field women rarely use the equal employment opportunity counseling system to pursue sex-based complaints. When they must fight to progress, women turn to those closest to them—to other women (including office workers), to their boss and male co-workers, and to other key supporters. Increasingly there is a feminist climate of support for women field workers. Empirical trends in the organization of forestry work, agency policy, and the family status of woods-working women also condition the eventual acceptance of women in the woods.

The future of women field workers in the Forest Service ultimately reflects the juncture of history and biography. Great tolerance, skill, and commitment are demanded of them as they cross dangerous borders and challenge old ways. Yet the future of every eager woman who comes on board with the coming of spring is shaped too by the sex structure of the organization she joins, by the particular historical and political moment—and by particular people too.

7

Conclusion

During the 1970s an impressive array of all-male sanctuaries faced challenge, not only at work but in sport and the arts, in schoolrooms and clubrooms. The far-reaching implications of these early forays outweigh their limited scope. Even a handful of women fire fighters or priests raise large questions for ever-larger audiences, altering the terms of public debate and sentiment. The experiences of women integrating men's jobs command considerable public attention for what they suggest of insurgency and counterinsurgency and for future generations of women workers. Sociologically, these pioneers help us grasp the dynamic of the assignment by sex of challenge and opportunity—now so evidently and painfully structuring our work and personal lives.

Effective challenge to the sexual division of labor hinges on understanding and analysis, grounded in close study of even the smallest changes. Thus the first intention and accomplishment of this work follows the style and spirit of the documentary. Only rarely do outsiders learn the inside story, or glimpse the private risks and rewards of women on the front lines of challenge to traditional barriers. Rendering an accurate portrayal of this new social territory topped the agenda in constructing this account of woods-working women and men.

Women field workers are both the changers and the changed. On the trails and around the shop we see them learn new ways of working and relating as they launch new careers. In ways subtle and stark, they in turn alter the status quo of the male workplace. Women's presence in the previously all-male work world is never unmeaningful, however limited. When co-workers are unmistakably and unavoidably female, new issues suddenly complicate routines of work and companionship. Both women and men in this study share a heightened sensitivity to issues of gender and work as they learn to work together.

The portrait is necessarily incomplete, for in any inquiry only certain questions are asked and answered. Through all stages of the study, the underlying question remained the original one: Can we see, in the moment of change, factors maintaining and undermining the sex-segregated workplace? By examining one particularly masculine occupation experiencing even limited sexual integration we hoped to see more clearly the grounds of resistance to women as well as the conditions of their acceptance. The burden of analysis has been to convey the tremendous reservoir of both support and resistance to women in the woods, and to illustrate the impact of this contradiction on the daily lives of women and men at work. We have seen some of the ways women influence work and workplace, have traced the persistence of male privilege and traditional patterns in the face of female insurgency, and have explored the tangled roots of sexuality at work.

The final image must be of struggle and uncertainty. In daily work life, we find that male co-workers do attempt control over female integration through a variety of mechanisms, principally by: sexualizing the workplace culture; cultivating sexual or quasi-sexual relations with women co-workers; sexual harassment and abuse; elaborating a sexual division of labor ensuring male dominance; asserting formal and informal authority through supervision and training; defining specific models of accommodation for women newcomers.

In these ways male workers defend the status quo and hence male privilege and dominance. Male control is not monolithic, however. It faces challenge from determined women committed to an equitable future in forestry. In their account we see women drawing on a number of resources, principally: deemphasizing sexual themes at work; demonstrating competence and commitment; seeking male alliance and sponsorship; developing a repertoire of interpersonal tactics to control resistance; pursuing organizational avenues of redress; cultivating formal and informal networks of support between women.

These are the key resources of insurgency and counterinsurgency identified by this study of women in field work. The male effort to contain female entry strengthens gender differences and boundaries, reaffirming in the face of challenge many traditional patterns. Ironically, in some ways female newcomers also help maintain stereotypic relations as they begin working with men in the woods.

Challenging Conditional Acceptance

Most woods-working women work compatibly with most men, but their eventual acceptance comes within a context of continued male dominance. Boundaries to successful integration are imposed through male control over the sexual tenor of the workplace, the sexual division of labor, and appropriate models of interaction. At issue is the ambience of workplace culture as much as who receives what job training, and the role of sexuality as well as role models for women in the field.

This analysis suggests that, in the long run, conditional acceptance is the critical mechanism of male control confronting pioneering women and limiting the significance of workplace integration. In their determination to succeed, most women field workers accept the compromise.[1] They feel defensively impelled to conform, for they appear to "take the place of a man," entering the masculine workplace only at the pleasure of those who came first. Hence, they feel no legitimate right to help define the tenor of interaction enlivening the workplace or to set their own boundaries or conditions. In addition, they see all too clearly the consequences for women not conforming to this model of female integration. Traditional patterns in sexual interaction and the division of labor sometimes help women negotiate entry into unfamiliar territory, where old rules are the best guides. As token women they are isolated and vulnerable, increasing the personal cost of nonconformity.

Yet tolerance for the compromise of conditional acceptance strengthens male control over the terms of integration. It credits the claim to male prerogative in work, culture, and interaction, undermining the potential for new and invigorating ways for men and women to work together. Meaningful challenge to sexual segregation at work means more than opening the doors briefly for a privileged few to join in men's jobs on conventional terms. It means struggling over the terms of acceptance, lest women simply pass through—perhaps brightening the day for a few male workers but forfeiting a precious opportunity for change.

Challenging conditional acceptance is women field workers' essential yet difficult task, made especially difficult by the burdens of tokenism. In this case study of women in forestry, as in other accounts from the white-collar world, the significance of sexually unbalanced work groups cannot be overstated. A host of problems created by the stigma of sexuality and tokenism reside in the essential issue of number and proportion, quite as certainly for women lawyers, electricians, and woods workers.

The social condition of the token must be altered before effective challenge is possible to the male dominance of field work. Women in balanced and unbalanced groups move in fundamentally different worlds of opportunity, with different implications for organization and occupation. Confining women to stereotypic categories of work and co-worker is more difficult as women approach parity numerically. Performance pressures and the demands of the protection racket abate when attention is not always riveted on the female minority. Normalizing the explosive sexual imbalance may also undermine the tendency to sexualized interaction in the male-dominated workplace.

Perhaps most importantly, problems rooted in organizational structure can be addressed when women begin to experience the personal and collective strength of numbers. The solo woman cannot with impunity persist in asserting competence or pursuing complaints. A critical mass of women workers more effectively tackles those private troubles rooted in the process of change. Women in greater numbers may act with the confidence and support of other women. The support of women co-workers will be essential in the successful rejection of the terms of conditional acceptance.

The full impact of sexual integration has not been felt, for women field workers in the Forest Service are yet so marginal to the work force. If the future brings a more natural balance, the women and men who have spoken here of their days together in the woods may realize the satisfactions of fully sharing woods work and may enjoy the promise of new possibilities in the social relations of gender.

Methodological Appendix

The research upon which this work is based involved no direct financial commitment by the U.S. Forest Service, although it did demand some personnel time as well as limited use of agency franking privileges. The research design was approved by the appropriate local and national offices and by departmental and university Committees for the Protection of Human Subjects. An informed consent form was used in each interview. A brief summary statement of the major conclusions of the dissertation was prepared and distributed to study participants. It was subsequently reproduced by the agency and was distributed to management throughout Region VI.

Because of their small numbers, contact was attempted with each of the predominantly field-working women with permanent jobs in the two national forests selected for study. For comparison, a number of temporary women field workers were also included. Three-quarters of the fifty interviews were conducted with women in the larger of the two study forests. The overall response rate of 51 percent masks the substantially higher response from the core group (76 percent of all permanent women in the larger national forest) and reflects many difficulties experienced in contacting the mobile seasonal workers. Potential respondents were contacted indirectly by personnel employees because of agency provisions for employee privacy. The method of contact (postal cards indicating interest, to be returned to the researcher) left unclear whether the interview requests were received. The interviews were tape recorded and averaged two hours in length.

Of the eighteen unit managers in the two study forests, seven were selected for diversity of status and reputation, and each agreed to participate. Five of the six spouses or lovers contacted (again, for diversity of situation) agreed to be interviewed. A pool was defined of male co-workers identified by women as either particularly accepting or hostile, narrowed to reflect the variety of departments and districts. Of these, ten (61 percent) participated, including two of five men seen as very difficult.

An open-ended questionnaire was distributed to all equal employment opportunity counselors in both forests to augment the data with an insider's perspective on the counseling program, affirmative action, and sexual harassment. It was completed and returned by 60 percent (eleven), twice as often by those counselors in the larger forest.

Sample Description

In the group of women field workers interviewed, there are nineteen seasonal and thirty-one permanent workers, of whom four are professionals. But the lines are blurred: two temporaries, for example, have more than five years of consecutive experience, and almost all the permanent workers had at least one season as a temporary; several had as many as fifteen seasonal years. Both groups include women with strictly local experience and others with broad experience in other positions and other forests and regions. Both the confirmed "lifer" and the genuinely temporary worker are represented.

They are a fairly well-educated group of low-paid workers. Two-thirds have gone beyond high school and half of these have earned college degrees; one-quarter have taken the two-year associate degree in forestry. The sample includes eight women (17 percent) at or below a GS-3, four GS-7's (8 percent), and three GS-9's (6 percent); most are GS-4's (40 percent) and GS-5's (29 percent). While 84 percent of the temporary workers have completed at least two years of college, 90 percent are employed at or below a GS-4.

As a group, they are white and largely Anglo-Saxon Protestant. The average age is thirty, ranging from twenty to sixty-three. Temporary women average eight years younger than the modal thirty-four-year-old permanent worker. While half live with men, only three of the fifty have school-aged children. Three fairly distinct groups emerge: young, unattached women, temporary or permanent; their slightly older, married (or committed) counterparts, very few of whom have or plan families; and that group of older, married women with families now grown and independent. There are correspondingly clear differences of ambition, style, and politics.

They work in the first instance not for love of wildlife or timber but for money. Half are self-supporting, and of those living with men, well-off professional lovers and spouses are conspicuous by their absence. Half of the men in their lives work or worked until recently for the Forest Service, largely as lower-level technicians, and others work in some aspect of the timber industry. Despite nepotism regulations, Forest Service couples and families are not unusual.

By and large, this group of women comes from solidly middle- and lower-middle-class families, with technical fields and lower-status professional fathers well represented. Working-class backgrounds of woods work and the skilled trades were also common. Few were either the daughters of the wealthy or the marginally self-supporting, though there are instances of both extremes. More than half are from two-earner families. Many outdoor-working women remember their mothers as resourceful and determined figures. Class background is never more complicated than here, in assessing the impact of mothers' background and occupational and educational prospects on the class identity and life-style of the family. At any rate, we can conclude that the lines of influence from mother to daughter do not work in any direct, unambiguous fashion, for the vast majority held typically female positions when employed, and just under half of these mothers are remembered primarily as homemakers.

In order to flesh out the image of "the Forest Service boys" emerging from long conversations with their co-workers, a number of men were interviewed. In many respects they resemble the female sample, but there are differences worth noting. The fifteen male co-workers and supervisors include only two professionals and three temporary workers. They thus best represent the permanent technicians in the Forest Service, who are in fact those men field women will most likely meet. The sample is also weighted toward fire control, which employs six of the thirteen nonprofessionals. Job tenure ranges from more than twenty years to just one season, though most speak from considerable experience, both as temporaries and later as permanent workers. Among them are three GS-4's (20 percent), four each (27 percent) at the rank of GS-5 and GS-7, three GS-9's (20 percent), and one GS-11.

Half of this group of men are under thirty and half are older, and almost all are married or live with women. About half also have families, and in the majority of cases wives and lovers are employed, largely in traditional fields. Their own families of origin tended to be more traditional, including only a few employed mothers. Two-thirds of the men are veterans, of whom two were officers. Most had moved in and out of the Forest Service, the military, school, and jobs like tree planting, logging, and nursery and park work. Few had any prior experience working with women. Six are committed to the Forest Service way of life and work, while several periodically consider leaving, perhaps for contract forestry work in the private sector.

Taken together, these characteristics inform the statements, perceptions, and feelings of the women and men who joined in this portrait of sexual integration of field work in the Forest Service.

Notes

Preface

1. Seventy-two interviews were completed, including fifty with field-going women workers, seven with unit managers, and fifteen with male co-workers and supervisors, including five spouses or lovers also employed recently by the Forest Service in field jobs. See the methodological appendix for details of sample selection and description. Among both female and male samples, the principal kinds of work groups and workers are represented. Professionals and technicians, permanent and seasonal, old-timers, and beginners are all included, as are the dedicated and the disaffected. The various jobs, departments, and districts of the two study forests appear, though not systematically, and the tremendous diversity of style and future is tapped.

2. The small numbers of field-working women and the sociological intimacy of the ranger districts make key incidents, distinctive attitudes, or unique jobs clear keys to identity. In such cases, I take poetic license in rearranging circumstances or retelling incidents, though direct quotations are always correct. Preserving the authenticity of original sentiments and insights without sacrificing anonymity is essential to the work. It is here, and not in the details of a situation, that veracity is rooted.

1. Introduction

1. While the popular press abounds with impressionistic sketches of women in nontraditional jobs, few detailed studies are available of the actual process of integration taking place in male occupations. Among the exceptions are Rosabeth Moss Kanter's study of women in management, *Men and Women of the Corporation* (New York: Basic, 1977); Margaret Hennig and Ann Jardim, *The Managerial Woman* (New York: Anchor Press/Doubleday, 1978); Mary Lindenstein Walshok, *Blue-Collar Women* (New York: Anchor Press/Doubleday, 1981); and Cynthia Epstein, *Women's Place* (Berkeley: University of California Press, 1970). When women in nontraditional fields are considered, the familiar bias toward professional careers prevails, while sexual integration of blue-collar workplaces dominates empirically.

2. An extensive literature is available on the sex structure of the labor force. Particularly useful are Valerie Oppenheimer, *The Female Labor Force in the United States* (Berkeley: University of California Press, 1970); Edward Gross, "Plus Ça Change . . . ? The Sexual Structure of Occupations over Time," *Social Problems* 16 (Fall 1968): 198–208; Alice Kessler-Harris, "Stratifying by Sex: Understanding the History of Working Women," in R. Edwards, M. Reich, and D. Gordon, eds.,

154

Labor Market Segmentation (Lexington, Mass.: Heath, 1975); Martha Blaxall and Barbara Reagan, eds., *Women and the Workplace: The Implications of Occupational Segregation* (Chicago: University of Chicago Press, 1976); and Francine Blau, "The Data on Women Workers, Past, Present, and Future," in Ann Stromberg and Shirley Harkess, eds., *Women Working* (Palo Alto: Mayfield, 1978).

3. A rich literature is developing on these and other facets of the internal labor market. Some sources on these topics include: "The Occupations of Women," in Theodore Caplow, *The Sociology of Work* (Minneapolis: University of Minnesota Press, 1954); Rosabeth Moss Kanter, "Women and the Structure of Organizations," in R. Kanter and M. Millman, eds., *Another Voice: Feminist Perspectives on Social Life and Social Science* (New York: Doubleday, 1975); Joan Acker and Donald Van Houten, "The Sex Structure of Organizations: Selective Recruitment and Control," *Administrative Science Quarterly* 19 (June 1974): 152–162; Francine Blau, "Sex Segregation of Workers by Enterprise in Clerical Occupations," in R. Edwards, M. Reich, and D. Gordon, eds., *Labor Market Segmentation;* Cynthia Epstein, *Women's Place;* Michael Korda, *Male Chauvinism: How It Works* (New York: Random House, 1972); and Paul Goldman, "The Organizational Caste System and the New Working Class," *Insurgent Sociologist* 3 (Winter 1973): 41–51.

4. In my view, the socialist-feminist perspective, while still developing, is the most promising interpretation of the sexual stratification of the labor force. It looks at how women's lives are structured by the intersection of sex, race, and class and, in the largest sense, by both capitalism and patriarchy. For example, consider Heidi Hartmann's "Capitalism, Patriarchy, and Job Segregation by Sex," *Signs* 1 (Spring 1976): 137–169.

5. Employed women have historically been subject to sexual abuse or harassment on the job, from simple sexual innuendo to rape. Household servants in colonial America as well as black women under slavery and domestic workers today are highly visible victims of sexual abuse. See, respectively, Richard Morris, *Government and Labor in Early America,* excerpt in R. Baxandall, L. Gordon, and S. Reverby, eds., *America's Working Women* (New York: Vintage, 1976); Angela Davis, "Reflections on the Black Woman's Role in the Community of Slaves," *Black Scholar* 3 (December 1971): 3–15; David Katzman, "Domestic Service: Woman's Work," in A. Stromberg and S. Harkess, eds., *Women Working.* Firsthand accounts of working conditions during the development of industrial capitalism often touch on this subject, as do novels of the period, such as Dreiser's *Sister Carrie* or Louisa May Alcott's *Work.* Later, office work was to be defined as relatively clean, safe employment for respectable (middle-class, educated) white women, though modern portraits of the secretary emphasize sexual overtones. See Ann Gordon, Mari Jo Buhle, and Nancy Schrom, eds., "Women in American Society," *Radical America* 5 (July–August 1971): 1–69; and Nancy Morse, *Satisfaction in the White Collar Job* (Ann Arbor: University of Michigan Press, 1953). Also writing on the transformation of office work is Margery Davies, "Women's Place Is at the Typewriter: The Feminization of the Clerical Labor Force," *Radical America* 8 (July–August 1974): 1–28. On the secretary, see Mary Kathleen Benet, *The Secretarial Ghetto* (New York: McGraw-Hill, 1973). Prather's analysis of the bank teller job indicates how some occupations are quite deliberately sexualized and glamorized to en-

courage women workers. Jane Prather, "When the Girls Move In: A Sociological Analysis of the Feminization of the Bank Teller's Job," *Journal of Marriage and the Family* 33 (November 1971): 777–781. Some of the recent research on sexual harassment at work emphasizes the larger context of a sexualized workplace. See in particular Catharine MacKinnon, *Sexual Harassment of Working Women* (New Haven: Yale University Press, 1979).

6. Indeed, female employment of any kind was once considered morally suspect. Arguments were made for protective legislation in the classic 1908 *Muller* v. *Oregon* case, partly on the grounds that employment deadened women's higher sentiments while increasing their craving for "excitement and sensual pleasure." See Robert Smuts, *Women and Work in America* (New York: Schocken, 1971), pp. 118–119. Today, women workers are particularly suspect in settings involving extensive personal contact with men (as in mixed-sex crews), work demanding frequent overtime, night work or travel, and work done in isolated settings (from ranger districts to outer space). Hanna Papanek writes of Muslim societies that the fear for sexual morality so severely limits interaction between the sexes outside the home as to create the demand for a female professional elite to service women. See Papanek, "Purdah in Pakistan: Seclusion and Modern Occupations for Women," *Journal of Marriage and the Family* 33 (August 1971): 517–530. In India, nursing is considered inappropriate work for women because of the necessary intimate contact with male patients (Constantina Safilios-Rothschild, *Love, Sex, and Sex Roles* [Englewood Cliffs, N.J.: Prentice-Hall, 1977], p. 88). One study of ethnic variations in female employment patterns in the early 1900s finds that the sexual jealousy of the men of Buffalo's Italian community restricted the entry of their wives and daughters into the domestic and factory work popular among other ethnic groups (Virginia McLaughlin, "Patterns of Work and Family Organization: Buffalo's Italians," in M. Gordon, ed., *The American Family in Social-Historical Perspective* [New York: St. Martin's, 1973]). Such jealousy is also often suggested to account for the relatively low employment rates of Hispanic women, as in Elizabeth Almquist and Juanita Wehrle-Einhorn, "The Doubly Disadvantaged: Minority Women in the Labor Force," in A. Stromberg and S. Harkess, eds., *Women Working.*

7. Consider the women interviewed by Studs Terkel in *Working* (New York: Avon, 1972); Letty Cottin Progrebin's "The Intimate Politics of Working with Men," *Ms.* (October 1975): 48–51, 96, 105–106; or Terry Weatherby, *Conversations: Working Women Talk about Doing a Man's Job* (Millbrae, Calif.: Les Femmes Press, 1977). Weatherby's portraits indicate a high proportion of strikingly attractive women in nontraditional jobs, including former beauty queens. Recruiting for beauty may help cool opposition to women in male-dominated jobs, heightening for men the sexual possibilities of working relationships. Constantina Safilios-Rothschild is one sociologist who takes the issue of physical appearance seriously in the sexual integration of occupations ("Women and Work: Policy Implications and Prospects for the Future," in A. Stromberg and S. Harkess, eds., *Women Working*). She suggests that the image of the working woman, especially in the "decorative" occupations, can be "normalized" by hiring average-looking women. Conversely, she seems to urge an affirmative action search for attractive women in

nontraditional fields, to counter the stereotype that only unattractive women find employment in men's fields. The stereotype is a powerful one, as Campbell has documented in the case of women in the natural sciences: David Campbell, "The Clash between Beautiful Women and Science," in A. Theodore, ed., *The Professional Woman* (Cambridge, Mass.: Schenkman, 1971).

8. Michael Satchell, "Now Women Pilots Get Their Turn with the Airlines," *Parade* (June 25, 1978): 6–7.

9. Quoted by Joan McCullough, in "Thirteen Who Were Left Behind," *Ms.* (September 1973): 41–45. The nature of some workplaces (massage parlors, cocktail bars) fairly demands attractive women workers. Indeed, a 1960 survey of business, industrial, and service employers found that more than one-quarter required "sex appeal" from their office workers. The survey is reported in Valerie Oppenheimer, *The Female Labor Force in the United States*.

10. Heidi Hartmann provides a persuasive overview of male resistance in "Capitalism, Patriarchy, and Job Segregation by Sex." See also Stanley Aronowitz, *False Promises* (New York: McGraw-Hill, 1973); and Harry Braverman, *Labor and Monopoly Capital* (New York: Monthly Review Press, 1974).

11. Barbara Garson's portrait of workers develops the theme of protecting autonomy in any way possible. See *All the Livelong Day* (New York: Doubleday, 1977). Theodore Caplow writes on the significance of an "antifeminine" work culture, in low-wage occupations particularly, in *The Sociology of Work,* p. 242. See also Michael Cherry's *On High Steel* (New York: Ballantine, 1974) for a portrait of work with a vividly masculine culture. Male camaraderie provided by work (including language, humor, shared leisure activity, work-related sports or drinking, etc.) is very highly valued. Women's exclusion from this realm of affect and activity is one mechanism by which women are discouraged in male-dominated occupations. See Cynthia Epstein, *Women's Place,* for the case of the professions.

12. Typically, female occupations are closely supervised, with limited control over the productive process or working conditions and restricted advancement or reward. These general attributes can follow women entering new lines of work, affirming the negative image of women workers. The female worker, for example, continues to be suspected of high absentee and quit rates, although careful analysis indicates the relationship is spurious, reflecting not the character of female workers but the reaction of all workers to the kinds of low-level jobs most women hold. Kanter considers the evidence on this point, in "The Impact of Hierarchical Structure on the Work Behavior of Women and Men," *Social Problems* 23 (April 1976): 415–430. The U.S. Department of Labor published rebuttals of this and related myths as early as 1972. U.S. Department of Labor, Women's Bureau, "Facts about Women's Absenteeism and Labor Turnover," in Nona Glazer-Malbin and H. Y. Waehrer, eds., *Women in a Man-Made World* (Chicago: Rand McNally, 1972). Similarly, in the professions female entry has been linked to increased bureaucratization and centralization, thus lowering the status of the male fraternity. For example, see Amitai Etzioni, ed., *The Semiprofessions and Their Organizations* (New York: Free Press, 1969), introduction; and, in the same volume, Richard Simpson and Ida Harper Simpson, "Women and Bureaucracy in the Semi-Professions." Stereotypes about employed women

are easily confused with characteristics of typically female jobs. Pertinent arguments are reviewed by James Grimm, "Women in Female-Dominated Professions," in A. Stromberg and S. Harkess, eds., *Women Working;* and Cora Bagley Marrett, "Centralization in Female Organizations: Reassessing the Evidence," *Social Problems* 19 (Winter 1972): 348–357.

13. The Pacific Northwest Region (Oregon and Washington) enjoys within the Forest Service a reputation for leadership in minority hiring, and the two national forests selected for study share this reputation. One of the two recently rated second highest among the nineteen national forests in Region VI for proportionate minority hiring. Forest hiring is to reflect employment targets of the general 1990 affirmative action plan, and regular quarterly reports are now required at forest and regional levels. Both study forests participate actively in the Federal Women's Program, Equal Employment Opportunity (EEO) counseling, and advisory civil rights committees at every organizational level. The government is widely recognized locally as more open to women in field positions in forestry than are the local private concerns. Yet in 1970 in Oregon only 4 percent of all foresters were female. See Jan Newton and Sandra Gill, *Women Workers in Oregon: A Portrait in Time,* typescript (Eugene: University of Oregon Labor Education and Research Center, 1978).

2. The Context of Change

1. The very different experience of male integration of traditional female fields is discussed by James Grimm and Robert Stern, in "Social Relations and Internal Labor Market Structure: The Female Semi-professions," *Social Problems* 21 (June 1974): 690–705. See also Francine Blau, "The Data on Women Workers."

2. These and other generalizations in this section are based on observation and on interview material. The section also draws on Herbert Kaufman's analysis of the role of the forest ranger. This work also provides a more complete sketch of the organizational structure and national impact of the agency. See Herbert Kaufman, *The Forest Ranger* (Baltimore: John Hopkins University Press, 1960).

3. Data were provided by the Civil Rights staff of the Washington Office of the U.S. Forest Service.

4. Rosabeth Moss Kanter's comprehensive study of a major corporation analyzes the organizational and interpersonal consequences of women's token status in nontraditional jobs. Kanter suggests that the "two-token" situation is essentially identical to the classic, solo woman situation. Many of her observations are echoed here in this study of women woods workers. See Kanter, *Men and Women of the Corporation,* chap. 8, "Numbers: Minorities and Majorities." The difficulty for token women of supporting others is apparent whenever we look at women in nontraditional jobs. See, for example, Sally Hillsman Baker, "Women in Blue-Collar and Service Occupations," in A. Stromberg and S. Harkess, eds., *Women Working;* and Michelle Patterson and Laurie Engelberg, "Women in Male-Dominated Professions," in the same volume.

5. These figures are taken from data supplied by the Region VI Federal Women's Program coordinator. Although technical and administrative positions are treated as a single category in personnel data, this source is the best available indicator of women's entry into field work, most of which comes under the technical series. The inclusion of administrative positions means that these figures overstate somewhat the positive change in the proportion of female field workers.

6. Washington Office, Civil Rights Division, is the source for all nationwide personnel data used here.

7. Physically demanding work performed outdoors is the key to particularly masculine cultures in working-class occupations. In the Forest Service other factors also contribute, such as the enforced mobility of the labor force and work communities in very isolated regions, both of which demand accommodating and supportive families. The literature of the profession emphasizes these aspects of the job, along with its physical rigors, in warning all but the hardiest men away. See Hardy Shirley, *Forestry and Its Career Opportunities* (New York: McGraw-Hill, 1952), and Herbert Kaufman, *The Forest Ranger*. In contrast, for a comic sketch of the Forest Service worker, written with biting wit by an old-time logger, see Paul Hosmer, *Now We're Loggin'* (Portland: Metropolitan Press, 1930).

8. For analysis of the contribution of the spirit of homosociability to maintaining sex segregation, see Jean Lipman-Blumen, "Toward a Homosocial Theory of Sex Roles: An Explanation of the Sex Segregation of Social Institutions," *Signs* (Spring 1976): 15–32.

9. Kaufman's analysis of the district ranger in the Forest Service stresses trends toward disunity in the agency structure and hence the importance of cultural homogeneity and professional socialization to counteract these trends. Whether pressures to conform are greater here than in similar organizations is an empirical question. This research does confirm the importance of "fitting in" for organizational success, which creates special problems for women outsiders in this very male-dominated and masculine field. See particularly chap. 6 in Kaufman, *The Forest Ranger*.

10. Like their male counterparts, most of the women interviewed were Westerners by birth or sentiment. Many were reared on or near a farm, ranch, or rural suburban home or had passed important parts of childhood years at play in camp, in nearby parks, or on summer visits to country relatives. Whether Vermont skiers or Oregon joggers, they shared a common regard for the natural world and for outdoor activity; many were regular ball players, swimmers, or hikers. Early attraction to physical activity, even tomboyishness, is one "pattern-breaking" aspect of the lives of women in blue-collar jobs, interviewed by Walshok in *Blue-Collar Women*.

11. Most of the women interviewed grew up with brothers around the house, and for some this male presence mattered, limiting their opportunity to explore nontraditional home chores or hobbies. Women with sisters alone more often reported helping fathers with wood cutting or yard work, experience which later proved helpful. Some women, however, attributed their ease on male-dominated crews to early family experience with brothers.

3. Early Challenges and Opportunities

1. Some current data on the distribution by sex among key job categories are available for Region VI in 1981: foresters, 10 percent female; forest technicians, 13 percent; wildlife biologists, 31 percent; engineers, 4 percent; engineering technicians, 13 percent; landscape architects, 17 percent; soil scientists, 17 percent; range conservationists, 12 percent; hydrologists, 10 percent (data provided by the Civil Rights staff of the Washington office, U.S. Forest Service). It is worth bearing in mind that this region is particularly advanced in minority hiring.

2. Women workers dominate at the seed orchards and tree nurseries operated by the Forest Service to secure a supply of high-quality trees for replanting. Local housewives recruited during World War II seemed ideal workers—stable, responsible, and grateful for well-paid part-time work. At this time, women also began to replace men in the remote fire lookout towers. Year after year, local women return as "temporaries" to nursery jobs, which resemble outdoor factory work, manual and semiskilled. Their work keeps them in the cold and wet as they transplant and cultivate tiny seedlings. Later, it demands grueling shifts at the conveyor belt as the small trees are packaged for delivery to tree-planting crews. They earn the higher wages of the wage-grade scale, for doing the manual labor of men under conditions many men refuse. They work in a virtual female ghetto, supervised always by men until recently (and men still supervise at the highest levels). They may be joined by an occasional male worker waiting for good steady work elsewhere. Here too upward mobility is truncated, and there is little transition from nursery work to other district or zone jobs. Veterans' preference and high unemployment rates bring more men to these jobs currently, and the sexual mix in the nurseries now shows signs of change.

3. This "power multiplier" effect of gender on organizational status is evident in many ways. In their article, Acker and Van Houten consider the enhanced control, by virtue of gender, available to male mechanics relative to the female line workers in a tobacco factory, originally analyzed by Michael Crozier in *The Bureaucratic Phenomenon* (Chicago: University of Chicago Press, 1964). See Acker and Van Houten, "The Sex Structure of Organizations."

4. In Walshok's study of blue-collar pioneers, one-half of the women interviewed report at least some positive relationships with co-workers and supervisors, although only 31 percent note especially helpful bosses. In their second year on the job, 45 percent were able to report helpful supervisors, but another 39 percent noted particularly antagonistic supervisors (Mary Walshok, *Blue-Collar Women*, p. 220).

5. Organizations may vary internally in typical authority systems, for people bring with them to work their latent social identity, including sexual status, to which organizations are not indifferent. The point was made early on by Alvin Gouldner, both theoretically and empirically. See his "Organizational Analysis," in R. Merton, L. Broom, and L. Cottrell, Jr., eds., *Sociology Today* (New York: Basic, 1959), and his empirical study, *Patterns of Industrial Bureaucracy* (New York: Free Press, 1954). Even within highly bureaucratic organizations, women may be

subject to more paternalistic forms of authority. One study of women in professional work organizations finds patterns of "irrationality" in the treatment of women within otherwise very bureaucratic organizations. See Jon Miller and Sanford Labovitz, "Inequities in Organizations: Experiences of Men and Women," *Social Forces* 54 (December 1975): 365–379. Kanter explores analytically the paternalistic control of women at work so evident in portraits of working women. See Kanter, "Women and the Structure of Organizations," and Elinore Langer, "The Women of the New York Telephone Company," *New York Review of Books,* vol. 14, nos. 5–6 (March 12, 26, 1970): 14–22.

6. Supervisors can occasionally recommend cash awards for outstanding performance. One woman complained that her reward for special effort was merely a lunch out with her boss, although cash awards were not uncommon in her district and department. Sexist forms of reward and control in organizations were examined by Acker and Van Houten in their review of the early Hawthorne studies (see "The Sex Structure of Organizations").

7. It has been estimated that as much as 80 percent of the job is learned informally from co-workers in crafts jobs. Sally Hillsman Baker, "Women in Blue-Collar and Service Occupations," p. 366. Difficulty in securing proper training from co-workers and bosses is a major obstacle reported by virtually every study of women in nontraditional fields. It is particularly acute in the skilled trades and crafts, where the apprenticeship system institutionalizes informal peer learning, as Walshok discovers in *Blue-Collar Women.*

8. Whyte's early analysis of sexual status in restaurants documents the resistance of men to women able to initiate lines of action for them. Male cooks, for example, introduced spindles for food orders in order to mediate the direct control of waitresses over their own work. Turning female supervisors into informal straw bosses is a similar mechanism of adaptation to inappropriate female authority (William F. Whyte, "The Social Structure of the Restaurant," *American Journal of Sociology* 54 [January 1949]: 302–310).

9. The integration of women in forestry may proceed differently in some respects outside the Forest Service and other public natural resource agencies. Production pressures in private-sector forest products firms may increase opposition to women initially. The trend to contract work in the Forest Service may enhance the difference between public and private forestry work. Should Forest Service work become more bureaucratic, professional, and "feminized," a new hierarchy may develop within forestry: low-wage, low-status government workers (largely female) inspecting the contract work of high-wage, high-status private sector workers (largely male). A change of this magnitude will be very slow in developing, however.

4. Shoulder to Shoulder: Models of Accommodation

1. In this discussion of the visibility and vulnerability of the token, we see some of the pressures of the social management of stigma as discussed originally by

Erving Goffman and as applied to women professionals by Cynthia Epstein. See Erving Goffman, *Stigma: Notes on the Management of Spoiled Identity* (Englewood Cliffs, N.J. Prentice-Hall, 1963), and Cynthia Epstein, *Women's Place.*

2. Many women with experience at fire camp complained of the lack of separate shower facilities for women. Certain hours are set for women to use camp showers in some cases; the hours are either insufficient or conflict with sleeping hours or duty shifts. This is a real issue for fire fighters when fires stretch on for weeks, and it strikes some women as a petty form of harassment.

3. Fears of fire fighters "buggering in the bushes" if women attend project fire camp have largely abated, and the sexual activity that does occur is most often attributed instead to non–Forest Service women, or at least to non-field-working women. Those with personal experience laugh at the very idea of sex after a long day spent building a fire line.

4. One study found that female deference to men at work was central to male managers' acceptance of women in the workplace. See Bernard Bass, J. Krusell, and R. Alexander, "Male Managers' Attitudes toward Working Women," *American Behavioral Scientist* 15 (November–December 1971): 221–236.

5. Very early, Hacker outlined a variety of accommodation techniques characteristically adopted by women around men, as is evident in this portrait of social relations at work. See Helen Mayer Hacker, "Women as a Minority Group," *Social Forces* 30 (October 1951): 60–69. More recently, Kanter has written on the "role traps" the token position forces upon women as they struggle to relate to the relentless stereotyping that surrounds them. This research illustrates how very much of a trap these models of accommodation can become. See chap. 8 in Kanter's *Men and Women of the Corporation.*

6. One study of women and men entering sex-atypical occupations suggests that male newcomers also experience fairly high levels of stress, performance pressures, and similar bouts of testing and teasing. Interestingly, the female "host group" questioned the sexual preference of the male newcomers, linking deviant job choice to "deviant" sexuality—although their first assumption was that male newcomers were motivated primarily by the prospect of rapid career development. See Carol Schreiber, *Changing Places: Men and Women in Transitional Occupations* (Cambridge, Mass.: M.I.T. Press, 1979), p. 77.

5. Sexual Relations of Production

1. Caplow's early discussion of the occupations of women is remarkable for its attention to sexuality at work. He notes the importance of women's physical appearance, asserts that the jealousy of spouses can hinder integration, and suggests that inevitable sexual or quasi-sexual relations at work detract from the cohesiveness and thus the productivity of small work groups; see *The Sociology of Work.* Recent attention to sexual harassment in the workplace and to the organizational management of romance and attraction expands the boundaries of sociological interest in the workplace. See, for example, D. Neugarten and J.

Shafritz, eds., *Sexuality in Organizations: Romantic and Coercive Behaviors at Work* (Oak Park, Ill.: Moore, 1979).

2. Rose Laub Coser, "Laughter among Colleagues: A Study of the Social Functions of Humor among the Staff of a Mental Hospital," *Psychiatry* 23 (1960): 81–95.

3. As MacKinnon writes in her analysis of sexual harassment, the sexualizing of the workplace makes a woman, by virtue of her very presence, a "provocative anomoly" in many workplaces. See MacKinnon, *Sexual Harassment of Working Women.*

4. Many of these themes emerge in other contexts as well, as for instance in the white-collar business organization intensively studied by Kanter. Her analysis of the token status suggests that the presence of women acts to heighten dominant cultural boundaries, such as exaggerated discussion of physical prowess or sexual adventures. In this way, too, sexualized work relations and workplace culture reinforce the sense of difference and distance so striking in this study of women woods workers. See Kanter, *Men and Women of the Corporation,* pp. 222–224.

5. Only one systematic study probes this dimension of the sexual relations of production. Interestingly, many of its insights appear in Korda's semidocumentary discussion of the world of magazine publishing as well as in such fictional treatments of office work as Joseph Heller's *Something Happened.* See Michael Korda, *Male Chauvinism,* and Robert Quinn, "Coping with Cupid: The Formation, Impact, and Management of Romantic Relationships in Organizations," *Administrative Science Quarterly* 22 (March 1977): 30–45. The study is limited to third-party reports, primarily by white, middle-class professional men (71 percent of the respondents were male), and it considers only professional or semiprofessional organizations.

6. The Quinn study focuses on the organizational consequences of workplace romances. Most affairs (generally the boss-secretary pair) were known to co-workers (though those involved steadfastly believed them secret), and the most commonly reported impact was an increased level of gossip. The main behavioral changes reported were "favoritism" benefiting the lovers and a slightly higher level of distraction on the men's part. Significantly most affairs ended with the firing or transfer of those women involved, often by their erstwhile lovers and boss (Quinn, "Coping with Cupid").

7. In the Quinn study, women more often than men were seen as engaged in an instrumental relationship benefiting them professionally in terms of expanded work responsibility, control over access to key people (the lover), and enhanced organizational power. This pattern parallels the suggestion of organizational analyst David Mechanic some years ago that personal attractiveness can be a power resource for lower-level organization members. See David Mechanic, "Sources of Power to Lower-Level Participants," *Administrative Science Quarterly* 7 (December 1962): 349–364. In the Forest Service, as in other organizations, stories of women's self-interested sexual relationships with more powerful men can readily be heard. Men more often than women, who remain skeptical, note instances of women who "use their sex" to land field jobs. Regardless of the actual

frequency of such job awards (which empirical research can never hope to establish), the speculation can be devastating.

8. A Federal Women's Program survey in the larger study forest in 1977 suggests the extent of sexual harassment for women office and field workers. Sexual harassment at work (undefined) was reported by 44 percent; of those, 65 percent specified verbal, 4 percent physical, and 31 percent both verbal and physical harassment. Of the 100 respondents, approximately half were clerical workers and one-third were seasonal workers. The Walshok study of women in blue-collar jobs reports that one-third of the sample have experienced harassment at work. See *Blue-Collar Women*. In a national survey conducted by *Redbook* magazine, more than 70 percent of the responding readers reported prior experience with sexual harassment. See Claire Safran, "What Men Do to Women on the Job," *Redbook* (November 1976): 149, 217–224. Some of the better contemporary work on sexual harassment includes the following: Catharine MacKinnon, *Sexual Harassment of Working Women;* Lin Farley, *Sexual Shakedown: The Sexual Harassment of Women on the Job* (New York: McGraw-Hill, 1978); Mary Bularzik, "Sexual Harassment at the Workplace: Historical Notes," *Radical America* 14 (June 1978): 25–41; Peggy Crull, "The Impact of Sexual Harassment on the Job: A Profile of the Experiences of Ninety-two Women," in Neugarten and Shafritz, eds., *Sexuality in Organizations;* Peggy Crull, "Sexual Harassment and Male Control of Women's Work," *Women: Journal of Liberation* 8 (1982): 3–7; Karen Lindsey, "Sexual Harassment on the Job," *Ms.* (November, 1977): 47–52; Letty Cottin Pogrebin, "Sex Harassment," *Ladies' Home Journal* (June 1977): 24–28; Caryl Rivers, "Sexual Harassment: The Executive's Alternative to Rape," *Mother Jones* (June 1978): 21–29.

6. The Limits to Integration

1. Virtually all of the blue-collar women interviewed by Walshok reported initial harassment from male co-workers. When asked about negative aspects of their jobs, just under one-half specified "uncooperative, indifferent, and sometimes downright hostile relationships" with male co-workers. Walshok, *Blue-Collar Women*, p. 188. One study probes just this topic, surveying a major corporation in the process of desegregating major job categories; it includes 101 blue-collar women in previously male crafts jobs. Of these, 30 percent reported that male co-workers "gave them a hard time on the job," a figure they note may be artificially low because of lack of data on women who quit, a problem common to all studies of job satisfaction, including this one of women woods workers. Their study confirms others in establishing distinct patterns of male harassment in the experience of a very sizable minority of women pioneers. They note too that the majority report some level of eventual acceptance by male co-workers. As in this study, the two responses to women in men's jobs are not mutually exclusive or unidimensional. See Brigid O'Farrell and Sharon Harlan, "Craftworkers and

Clerks: The Effect of Male Co-Worker Hostility on Women's Satisfaction with Non-Traditional Jobs," *Social Problems* 29 (February 1982): 252–265.

2. Job success and co-worker acceptance cannot be assumed identical. Resistance toward those women newcomers who enjoy successful careers in other respects is part of what has been called the "cold war" against successful women. Safilios-Rothschild writes on the isolation and hostility toward the successful token woman in her article "Women and Work: Policy Implications and Prospects for the Future." One empirical study of successful professional women found that as women rose in the hierarchy, the inner sanctum of personal influence always remained one step removed. Paradoxically, the most successful women were also the most alienated, cut off from the informal networks of the organization. See Jon Miller and Sanford Labovitz, "Inequities in Organizations: Experiences of Men and Women."

3. Although general strategies of accommodation are obvious in most studies of women newcomers (for example, overachievement or efforts at social invisibility), we know little of the most successful specific interpersonal techniques adopted by women negotiating these tricky waters. A few firsthand accounts are suggestive. See the interview with the advertising writer in Studs Terkel, *Working,* or Gubbay's account of "waitressing" in a strip joint (Michele Gubbay, "The Paradise Lounge: Working as a Cocktail Waitress," in Baxandall, Gordon, and Reverby, eds., *America's Working Women*).

4. Also relevant is growing concern over women woods workers' exposure to health-threatening pesticides in forestry work. One woman included in this study has taken the issue to management, and several field-going women were reported to have quit their jobs rather than risk harm to their reproductive potential. A good source on health hazards of women's work is Jeanne Mager Stellman, *Women's Work, Women's Health* (New York: Pantheon, 1977).

5. Interestingly, the Walshok sample of blue-collar women in the crafts and trades is also heavily weighted toward the unmarried and toward people without young children at home. The women in crafts jobs in the O'Farrell and Harlan sample are also less likely to be married than the clerical sample these writers also surveyed. While women pioneers are unrepresentative of the general female labor force in this way and others, they are unlikely to remain so.

7. Conclusion

1. Easy acceptance of familiar ways of relating (e.g., as mascot, or mother, or ladylike buddy) is one strategy adopted by women and other outsiders in uneasy social circumstances. As Kanter writes, stereotyping the token and conforming to the stereotypes make things easier all around. Walshok adds that in her sample the most successful pioneers had the "work savvy" to blend into the prevailing workplace culture, however sexist. While she regrets the implications for women,

she concludes, "In order to cut it, you have to go with the norms of the dominant group" (Walshok, *Blue-Collar Women,* p. 232). At the risk of appearing to blame the victim, my own analysis suggests that challenging these boundaries is an important part of the job for women in nontraditional jobs if these jobs and workplaces are to become fully desegregated. Perhaps the issue is one of short- or long-term strategy.

Bibliography

Acker, Joan, and Donald Van Houten
1974 "The Sex Structure of Organizations: Selective Recruitment and Control." *Administrative Science Quarterly* 19 (June): 152–162.

Almquist, Elizabeth, and Juanita Wehrle-Einhorn
1978 "The Doubly Disadvantaged: Minority Women in the Labor Force." In A. Stromberg and S. Harkess, eds., *Women Working*. Palo Alto: Mayfield.

Aronowitz, Stanley
1973 *False Promises*. New York: McGraw-Hill.

Baker, Sally Hillsman
1978 "Women in Blue-Collar and Service Occupations." In A. Stromberg and S. Harkess, eds., *Women Working*. Palo Alto: Mayfield.

Bass, Bernard, Judith Krusell, and Ralph Alexander
1971 "Male Managers' Attitudes toward Working Women." *American Behavioral Scientist* 15 (November–December): 221–236.

Benet, Mary Kathleen
1973 *The Secretarial Ghetto*. New York: McGraw-Hill.

Blau, Francine
1975 "Sex Segregation of Workers by Enterprise in Clerical Occupations." In R. Edwards, M. Reich, and D. Gordon, eds., *Labor Market Segmentation*. Lexington, Mass.: Heath.
1978 "The Data on Women Workers, Past, Present, and Future." In A. Stromberg and S. Harkess, eds., *Women Working*. Palo Alto: Mayfield.

Blaxall, Martha, and Barbara Reagan, eds.
1976 *Women and the Workplace: The Implications of Occupational Segregation*. Chicago: University of Chicago Press.

Braverman, Harry
1974 *Labor and Monopoly Capital*. New York: Monthly Review Press.

Bularzik, Mary
1978 "Sexual Harassment at the Workplace: Historical Notes." *Radical America* 14 (June): 25–41.

Campbell, David
1971 "The Clash between Beautiful Women and Science." In A. Theodore, ed., *The Professional Woman*. Cambridge, Mass.: Schenkman.

Caplow, Theodore
1954 *The Sociology of Work*. Minneapolis: University of Minnesota Press.

Cherry, Michael
1974 *On High Steel: The Education of an Ironworker*. New York: Ballantine.

Coser, Rose Laub
1960 "Laughter among Colleagues: A Study of the Social Functions of Humor among the Staff of a Mental Hospital." *Psychiatry* 23 (February): 81–95.

Crull, Peggy
1979 "The Impact of Sexual Harassment on the Job: A Profile of Ninety-two Women." In D. Neugarten and J. Shafritz, eds., *Sexuality in Organizations: Romantic and Coercive Behaviors at Work*. Oak Park, Ill.: Moore.
1982 "Sexual Harassment and Male Control of Women's Work." *Women: A Journal of Liberation* 8: 3–7.

Davies, Margery
1974 "Women's Place Is at the Typewriter: The Feminization of the Clerical Labor Force." *Radical America* 8 (July–August): 1–28.

Epstein, Cynthia
1970 *Women's Place*. Berkeley: University of California Press.

Etzioni, Amitai, ed.
1969 *The Semi-professions and Their Organization*. New York: Free Press.

Farley, Lin
1978 *Sexual Shakedown: The Sexual Harassment of Women on the Job*. New York: McGraw-Hill.

Garson, Barbara
1977 *All the Livelong Day*. New York: Doubleday.

Goffman, Erving
1963 *Stigma: Notes on the Management of Spoiled Identity*. Englewood Cliffs, N.J.: Prentice-Hall.

Goldman, Paul
1973 "The Organizational Caste System and the New Working Class." *Insurgent Sociologist* 3 (Winter): 41–51.

Gordon, Ann, Mari Jo Buhle, and Nancy Schrom
1971 "Women in American Society: An Historical Contribution." *Radical America* 5 (July–August): 1–69.

Gouldner, Alvin
1954 *Patterns of Industrial Bureaucracy*. New York: Free Press.
1959 "Organizational Analysis." In R. Merton, L. Broom, and L. Cottrell, Jr., eds., *Sociology Today*. New York: Basic.

Grimm, James
1978 "Women in Female-Dominated Professions." In A. Stromberg and S. Harkess, eds., *Women Working*. Palo Alto: Mayfield.

Grimm, James, and Robert Stern
1974 "Social Relations and Internal Labor Market Structure: The Female Semi-professions." *Social Problems* 21 (June): 690–705.

Gross, Edward
1968 "Plus Ça Change . . . ? The Sexual Structure of Occupations over Time." *Social Problems* 16 (Fall): 198–208.

Gubbay, Michele
1976 "The Paradise Lounge: Working as a Cocktail Waitress." In R. Baxandall, L. Gordon, and S. Reverby, eds., *America's Working Women*. New York: Vintage.

Hacker, Helen Mayer
1951 "Women as a Minority Group." *Social Forces* 30 (October): 60–69.
Hartmann, Heidi
1976 "Capitalism, Patriarchy, and Job Segregation by Sex." *Signs: A Journal of Women in Culture and Society* 1 (Spring): 137–169.
Hennig, Margaret, and Ann Jardim
1978 *The Managerial Woman.* New York: Anchor Press/Doubleday.
Hosmer, Paul
1930 *Now We're Loggin'.* Portland: Metropolitan Press.
Kanter, Rosabeth Moss
1975 "Women and the Structure of Organizations." In R. Kanter and M. Millman, eds., *Another Voice: Feminist Perspectives on Social Life and Social Science.* New York: Doubleday.
1976 "The Impact of Hierarchical Structure on the Work Behavior of Women and Men." *Social Problems* 23 (April): 415–430.
1977 *Men and Women of the Corporation.* New York: Basic.
Katzman, David
1978 "Domestic Service: Woman's Work." In A. Stromberg and S. Harkess, eds., *Women Working.* Palo Alto: Mayfield.
Kaufman, Herbert
1960 *The Forest Ranger.* Baltimore: Johns Hopkins University Press.
Kessler-Harris, Alice
1975 "Stratifying by Sex: Understanding the History of Working Women." In R. Edwards, M. Reich, and D. Gordon, eds., *Labor Market Segmentation.* Lexington, Mass.: Heath.
Korda, Michael
1972 *Male Chauvinism: How It Works.* New York: Random House.
Langer, Elinore
1970 "The Women of the New York Telephone Company." *New York Review of Books*, vol. 14, nos. 5–6 (March 12, 26): 14–22.
Lindsey, Karen
1977 "Sexual Harassment on the Job." *Ms.* (November): 47–52, 74–76.
Lipman-Blumen, Jean
1976 "Toward a Homosocial Theory of Sex Roles: An Explanation of the Sex Segregation of Social Institutions." *Signs* 1 (Spring): 15–31.
MacKinnon, Catharine
1979 *Sexual Harassment of Working Women.* New Haven: Yale University Press.
McCullough, Joan
1973 "Thirteen Who Were Left Behind." *Ms.* (September): 41–45.
McLaughlin, Virginia
1973 "Patterns of Work and Family Organization: Buffalo's Italians." In M. Gordon, ed., *The American Family in Social-Historical Perspective.* New York: St. Martin's.
Marrett, Cora Bagley
1972 "Centralization in Female Organizations: Reassessing the Evidence." *Social Problems* 19 (Winter): 348–357.

Mechanic, David
   1962   "Sources of Power to Lower-Level Participants." *Administrative Science Quarterly* 7 (December): 349–364.
Miller, Jon, and Sanford Labovitz
   1975   "Inequities in Organizations: Experiences of Men and Women." *Social Forces* 54 (December): 365–379.
Morris, Richard
   1976   *Government and Labor in Early America* (1946). Excerpt in R. Baxandall, L. Gordon, and S. Reverby, eds., *America's Working Women.* New York: Vintage.
Morse, Nancy
   1953   *Satisfaction in the White Collar Job.* Ann Arbor: University of Michigan Press.
Neugarten, D., and J. Shafritz, eds.
   1979   *Sexuality in Organizations: Romantic and Coercive Behaviors at Work.* Oak Park, Ill.: Moore.
Newton, Jan, and Sandra Gill
   1978   *Women Workers in Oregon: A Portrait in Time.* Typescript. Eugene: University of Oregon Labor Education and Research Center.
O'Farrell, Brigid, and Sharon Harlan
   1982   "Craftworkers and Clerks: The Effect of Male Co-worker Hostility on Women's Satisfaction with Non-Traditional Jobs." *Social Problems* 29 (February): 252–265.
Oppenheimer, Valerie Kincaid
   1970   *The Female Labor Force in the United States.* Population Monograph Series 5. Berkeley: University of California Press.
Papanek, Hanna
   1971   "Purdah in Pakistan: Seclusion and Modern Occupations for Women." *Journal of Marriage and the Family* 33 (August): 517–530.
Patterson, Michelle, and Laurie Engelberg
   1978   "Women in Male-Dominated Professions." In A. Stromberg and S. Harkess, eds., *Women Working.* Palo Alto: Mayfield.
Pogrebin, Letty Cottin
   1975   "The Intimate Politics of Working with Men." *Ms.* (October): 48–51, 96, 105–106.
   1977   "Sex Harassment." *Ladies' Home Journal* (June): 24–28.
Prather, Jane
   1971   "When the Girls Move In: A Sociological Analysis of the Feminization of the Bank Teller's Job." *Journal of Marriage and the Family* 33 (November): 777–781.
Quinn, Robert
   1977   "Coping with Cupid: The Formation, Impact, and Management of Romantic Relationships in Organizations." *Administrative Science Quarterly* 22 (March): 30–45.

Rivers, Caryl
    1978   "Sexual Harassment: The Executive's Alternative to Rape." *Mother Jones* (June): 21–29.
Safilios-Rothschild, Constantina
    1977   *Love, Sex, and Sex Roles.* Englewood Cliffs, N.J.: Prentice-Hall.
    1978   "Women and Work: Policy Implications and Prospects for the Future." In A. Stromberg and S. Harkess, eds., *Women Working.* Palo Alto: Mayfield.
Safran, Claire
    1976   "What Men Do to Women on the Job." *Redbook* (November): 149, 217–224.
Schreiber, Carol
    1979   *Changing Places: Men and Women in Transitional Occupations.* Cambridge, Mass.: M.I.T. Press
Shirley, Hardy
    1952   *Forestry and Its Career Opportunities.* New York: McGraw-Hill.
Simpson, Richard, and Ida Harper Simpson
    1969   "Women and Bureaucracy in the Semi-professions." In A. Etzioni, ed., *The Semi-professions and Their Organization.* New York: Free Press.
Smuts, Robert
    1971   *Women and Work in America.* New York: Schocken.
Stellman, Jeanne Mager
    1977   *Women's Work, Women's Health.* New York: Pantheon.
Terkel, Studs
    1972   *Working.* New York: Avon.
U.S. Department of Labor, Women's Bureau
    1972   "Facts about Women's Absenteeism and Labor Turnover." In N. Glazer-Malbin and Helen Young Waehrer, eds., *Women in a Man-Made World.* Chicago: Rand McNally.
Walshok, Mary Lindenstein
    1981   *Blue-Collar Women: Pioneers on the Male Frontier.* New York: Anchor Books/Doubleday.
Weatherby, Terry
    1977   *Conversations: Working Women Talk about Doing a Man's Job.* Millbrae, Calif.: Les Femmes Press.
Whyte, William Foote
    1949   "The Social Structure of the Restaurant." *American Journal of Sociology* 54 (January): 302–310.

Index

Accommodation techniques: physical ability and job attitude, 67–69; protection racket, 76; models of, 76–78, 147; the ladylike buddy, 78–85, 98, 138; using humor, 89–91; accepting sexualized workplaces, 96–98, 108; defining sexual harassment, 110; for control of male hostility, 126; challenging, 148, 165–166 (n. 1). *See also* Co-worker acceptance

Affirmative action, 1, 4, 5, 29, 75; Forest Service history, 13–14; for minorities, 14–15; study forest commitment, 15–18, 158 (n. 13); controversy over, 16–17. *See also* Forestry, Forest Service

Bathrooms, 25, 71, 91–93

Career counseling, 15, 41
Child care, 22, 143
Civil Service, 10, 29
Clerical workers, 4–5, 24, 107, 131; job mobility of, 25–27; relations with women woods workers, 128–129
Competence, 44, 73, 83, 121; job ratings, 39; interaction with attitude, 65–69; accepting male help, 69–75. *See also* Job training, Physical ability, Accommodation techniques
Contract work, 5, 9, 50, 139; female contract inspectors, 48–50
Co-worker acceptance: of women contract inspectors, 50; and stereotyped femininity, 84; male friendships, 101, 124; following hostility, 134–137; conditional acceptance, 137–138, 144, 148; of successful women, 165 (n. 2). *See also* Accommodation techniques. Supervisory relations

Co-worker affairs, 88, 99, 163 (n. 6, n. 7); at fire camp, 59, 162 (n. 3); job consequences of, 99–104; impact on crew, 104–105; organizational management, 105–107. *See also* Rumor, Sexualized work relations, Jealousy

Co-worker hostility: in fire control, 31, 61–62; denial of job training, 42–44; toward women supervisors, 45–47; defense of masculine workplace, 61–62, 85; role of physical ability, 66–67; factors conditioning, 118–121; women's responses, 122–127, 130, 134; change to acceptance, 134–137; comparative data, 164 (n. 1). *See also* Sexual harassment

Co-worker relations: informal division of labor, 32–33; impact of tokenism, 52–54, 69, 100; physical competition, 56; paternalism, 69–76; models of accommodation, 76–78; the ladylike buddy model, 78–85

Dual careers, 142–143

Equal employment opportunity counseling, 15, 131–132; sexual harassment cases, 116

Family: influence on field-going women, 11, 21–22; family plans, 142–143; background of sample, 151–152
Federal Women's Program, 15–16, 109, 118, 130–131, 164 (n. 8)